The Light in His Soul

I0807114

The Light in His Soul

Lessons from My Brother's Schizophrenia

Rebecca Schaper

with Gerald Everett Jones

GREYHAWK MEDIA

ATLANTA, GA

GreyHawk Media
3000 Old Alabama Road, Suite 119
Alpharetta, GA 30022
books@rebeccaschaper.com
www.rebeccaschaper.com

ISBN: 978-0-9992771-1-9

Library of Congress Control Number: 2017952089

Portions of this memoir are based on the documentary film *A Sister's Call* (2012) by Rebecca Schaper co-produced and directed by Kyle Tekiela (Tekiela Creative) for GreyHawk Films in association with Kartemquin Films. Photos in this book are adapted from the movie except as noted below.

Photo of Kim in chapter 16: Courtney Buchanan

Photo of Lauren in chapter 18: Gabe Simpson

Photo of the author: Marion Yarger-Ricketts

Copyeditor: Robin Quinn, Quinn's Word for Word

Proofreader: Mike Mollett

Cover and interior designer: Gary Palmatier, ideas-to-images.com

In Memory of Call

Beyond all I see through the eyes of my brother,
Call gave me the inspiration to write this book.

Contents

Prologue

In the South, Call is not uncommon as a man's name. It was my father's and my brother's. Also in that part of the country, inspired Christians talk about receiving *the call*—a call of duty, a call to action—an outright order from God. My brother Call Richmond Jr. was my call to action. He had been a cheerful but disturbed and misunderstood young man. One day not long after he'd dropped out of his last year of college, Call ran away from home and disappeared.

I found him twenty years later. His paranoid schizophrenia was not yet formally diagnosed. I knew right away that it was up to me to get him whatever help he needed.

This is our story.

Rather, this is my memoir of caring for—and learning from—Call.

As a society—as a community of law-abiding, cooperative citizens—we tend to think of mental illness as a disease to be managed, disruptive behavior to be minimized, perhaps even an embarrassment to be hidden away. (And there are still those who think of illness as Satan's possession of the weak or the wicked.)

The professional caregivers have trays full of drugs that, in clever combinations and dosages, may seem to be helpful. But, for the most part, today's pharmaceuticals suppress the symptoms but never heal the problem—nor the hurtful effects on other people. The result might be acceptable to the community because the patient is now compliant and seemingly self-sufficient. However, the nightmare they've been living is not extinguished. Their internal television show—the swirling perceptions and misperceptions in the mind—has just been temporarily switched off, or its volume control turned way down.

The average person rarely has reason to question perceptions that seem real. During our dreams, haven't we all wondered whether we're participating in a real event? But a hallucination is another thing altogether. Imagine being wide awake, reaching for a doorknob, and not knowing if it's a real object or a figment of your obsessively creative mind. You reach out and grasp it. The feedback through the nerves of your hand, the coolness of the metal, and the hard slickness of its surface make you think it's a real thing. You tighten your grip and turn it clockwise.

It is a real knob in a real door, the door to your bathroom. You're standing there because the pressure in your bladder is giving you the routine message that you need to relieve yourself.

Understand—and this might be difficult for you to take in at this point—you *know* you can't trust your judgment. You seldom know whether your perceptions are real or hallucinatory. And yet you are intelligent enough to know that there's a difference. From moment to moment, you don't trust yourself. You don't trust your judgment about whether you're sane or ill.

You don't even trust your decision to open a door.

But, in this case, it's a real handle on a real door to your own bathroom. And you decide to open it.

And on the other side of the door, you see an undulating carpet of insects or a nest of writhing snakes or the face of someone you don't recognize giving you a menacing look. It's not a horror movie, and you can't turn it off. It's the way you live, all day every day you're awake. Sometimes, you open the door and all you see is the commode full of feces you forgot to flush down. Other times, when you remember to take your meds, you're in a fog and you grope your way to the porcelain receptacle and you do your business like everyone else in town.

You summon your courage and walk back through that door.

Some family members and caregivers—including certain medical professionals—assume that people with mental illness can't know the difference between hallucinations and reality. That's true part of the time. The difference isn't always clear. There is that moment with your hand on the doorknob when all the boundaries of reality are blurred.

Nevertheless, some people who later present symptoms of mental illness may have had happy, clear-headed childhoods. My brother did. When things go wrong, these individuals know they have entered strange, dangerous territory. If they receive medication—and if it works—they may feel safer for a while. At those times, treatment plans might seem to succeed, but all too often the effects are not lasting. In certain cases, brain chemistry may change to shake off the drug-induced dullness, as if the once-overactive mind was desperate to outwit the boredom. The patient might just decide to help the process along by forgetting to take some pills.

Absent the medication and at other unpredictable times, the illness may have other effects—including extraordinary visions, insights, or abilities. These effects can seem superhuman, even traits of genius. Imagine the thrill of living at that level. The brain seeks to sustain that high, but the intensity is unbearable—with or without moderating drugs. Eventually, patients will lose that energy and perhaps fall into a depression because their mellowed state is not at all exciting.

They may wonder what they've done wrong to deserve such suffering.

We all wonder why misfortune strikes. Not necessarily what the afflicted person did wrong, but what flaw in us or in the scheme of things invites any manner of pain or suffering into our lives?

Call's illness was just one facet of my family's troubled history. Our mother, Mary Pennington Richmond, suffered from schizophrenia and committed suicide just before Call went missing. Our father, Call Richmond Sr., was a heroic World War II veteran who, to use the modern term for it, suffered from post-traumatic stress disorder (PTSD). Although Dad was outwardly a fully functional, even respected member of the community, he abused my mother emotionally and physically. And he secretly abused me emotionally and sexually. Years later, I was to learn he'd also molested my oldest daughter Kim. No one in the family suspected it until, in her college years, Kim developed acute anorexia.

Eleven years after my mother's suicide, my father killed himself. He'd been remarried briefly, but he said in a suicide note that he'd never been truly happy. And in that note, he hinted at his overwhelming sense of guilt for the bad things he'd done.

My coping with—and, yes, *learning from*—Call's schizophrenia became intertwined with all these events and their decades-long impacts.

I've heard it said that mental illness can be accompanied by special gifts. I don't know whether that's always the case, but I'm still discovering the depth of Call's spiritual sensitivity and insight.

I don't mean to scare you, and my intention is not to preach. Given this brief glimpse of my family life, you may be strongly tempted not to read further.

I'm here to tell you—and perhaps this is the reason Call shared his life with us—that misfortune, heartache, gifts, and blessings come from unexpected—and often unlikely—directions. Yes, at one level this is a book about coping with mental illness, along with the stress in the family that inevitably surrounds it. But at its heart, this memoir is the outpouring of my belief in the enduring beauty of human existence and the loud, clear message that, no matter what your challenge or hardship, in finding your endurance, you may also find purpose and joy.

Chapter 1

Call Returns

In the movies as in so many ancient stories, we think about the call coming as a blinding flash of light or a thundering command. Yet sometimes it's as soft as the purr of a ringing phone.

The call to me was indirect, not from my brother but from my mother-in-law Marge. She'd been the first to get it, hearing the call as the ringing of her doorbell.

One morning in 1997, she and her husband were cleaning out a large closet in their basement. She'd phoned the Haven of Rest, a local charity, to pick up their furniture donations. A crew came out, loaded up their truck, and drove off.

One of the men stayed behind, turned back, marched up to her front porch, and rang the bell.

"I'm Call" was all he said when she opened the door.

His tone was matter-of-fact. No malice, but also no joy. No embarrassed getting around to the point. No apology. And also no pleading. This man was simply stating a fact.

"Good grief, Call," Marge said. "You know Rebecca's been looking all over for you. Come on in, and we're going to get her on the phone." She tried to keep the emotion out of her voice. If somehow she upset him, maybe he'd turn around and disappear again.

"You know, it's been twenty years," she said cautiously.

After being missing for twenty years, one morning Call appeared on Marge's front porch, rang the bell, and announced simply, "I'm Call."

"Yes, I do know that," he replied. Then came the hint of a chuckle, and his round face lit up with a smile. "So, don't you think it's about time?"

Why had he walked in on Marge? I was the one who'd been looking desperately for him—for years. It wasn't that she didn't care. But I was his sister, and everyone in my immediate and extended family knew that I had—with or without their blessing—made finding him my mission, to the point of obsession.

Maybe the answer is that he was finally ready to be found. And there was Marge. She was living near Greenville, South Carolina, our hometown. My husband Jim and I were with our teenage daughters Kim and Lauren over 130 miles away in suburban Atlanta. One day all those years ago, it had been in Greenville where Call

"Good grief, Call," Marge said. "You know Rebecca's been looking all over for you. Come on in, and we're going to get her on the phone."

walked off, never to be seen or heard from by anyone we knew—until two decades later when he announced himself to Marge.

Her explanation was "I think maybe there was a plan Upstairs for that."

She phoned me and put him on.

Me, I screamed. I bawled. But my screams were yelps of pure joy.

I drove up to Greenville from my home near Atlanta the very next day. Call and I hugged for a long time. Words didn't come until later.

He was forty. His sandy hair was thinning. His face was puffy and red. His gray beard was all the way down to his waist. He weighed just 130 pounds. Call wasn't starving, but he was surely undernourished. A lit cheroot was stuck in his mouth. He didn't bother to remove it as he talked, which wasn't all that much. Our Call was a man of few words, then as later.

He didn't have to tell me in so many words that he'd been homeless, broken, and alone. After he came back, I made sure he had the basics—shelter, food, and medical care. But I wasn't sure, at this point, whether he was capable of living on his own. When I visited him, I clipped his toenails, which were a half-inch too long and must have made it uncomfortable to wear shoes. Neglecting his personal hygiene was an issue we would come to deal with, more or less constantly.

It was like I was staring at this ghost, this faint, lifeless resemblance of someone I knew a long time ago. But that ghost was my beloved brother Call. Right then and there, I knew in my heart that I would do everything I possibly could to bring him back to life.

My husband and daughters later admitted that, on Call's return, he'd scared them at first. But, like a wild animal that has stumbled onto a trail, Call was much more afraid of us—afraid of everyone, really—than we were of him. For my part, all I saw was the hurt in his soul.

It's hard to explain what it feels like to have someone back in your life after so many years. All these questions were going through my head: *Where have you been? Why didn't you just pick up the phone and call us? You have a family, and we love you.* It saddened me to think that he didn't seem to know that.

When I say Call was gone for twenty years, that's not strictly true. He'd be gone and out of touch for long stretches of time, but

It's hard to explain what it's like to have someone back in your life after so many years.

every now and then he'd make himself known. He might phone, for example. In those days, a person could call collect, asking a live operator to reverse the charges (which were relatively more expensive than now). The operator would come on the line first and announce the caller and his location, then ask if you'd be willing to pay for the call. Just two years after he'd left home, in 1979, Call phoned me collect when I was pregnant with Kim. He told me he knew how Mom died. When I asked how he was, he simply said he was okay and not to worry about him. Then he hung up.

In 1985, Call paid a surprise visit when the family was together at Dad's in Greenville for Christmas. That's when my widowed father was living in the house where we kids grew up, on Chanticleer Drive. Call had a bitter argument with Dad (I'm not sure about what) and left in a fury.

Three years after that incident, Call phoned me collect from St. Louis to ask why Dad's phone was disconnected. I had to tell him how Dad had died. I pleaded with him to return to us, and I bought him a bus ticket to Atlanta. Call did visit us for a short while, but then he abruptly disappeared again without saying where he was going.

By 1991 our younger brother David was married to Shari, and Call showed up at their house to see their new baby Amanda. Neither David nor I could guess how Call had found out about the birth or knew how to find them.

As I reflect on the years before Call and I were reunited, I realize that I had no idea then what the future would hold. I could not have imagined the hardships we'd go through together as we tried to get his condition stabilized. All the time he was gone, I just knew I had to keep searching for him. It became an all-consuming mission for me, even when others advised me to give up. After there were so many years with no word from him, some of Call's old friends tried to convince me that he must surely be dead.

When I thought about my searching for him, year after year, I wondered where my inner strength and determination came from. I began to suspect that it was because of this communication, this presence, that bound us together.

After the seeming miracle of Call's return to us, I began to believe that Marge was right—that, in some way, there was a plan for all of it. But I didn't think that God was moving us around like pieces on a chessboard. I was sure that I'd played an active part, and so had Call.

And in recent years, after more than a decade of trying to support Call, I have come to believe that he and I had a kind of *spiritual agreement*—that on some deep level we had decided to enrich each other's lives and to guide each other through significant life lessons. Eventually, I'd have a whole vocabulary for this faith I had in him, but it was an awareness that dawned slowly, and by a series of—what else would you call them?—*lessons.*

I'll have much more to say about how, in many ways, Call became *my* caregiver.

CHAPTER 2

I Take Responsibility for Call's Care

AFTER CALL RETURNED, I WANTED HIM TO HAVE THE CHANCE my parents never gave him. First, I had to see that he had a place to live, food on his table, and professional care.

I wanted to take him home with me, to install him someplace near where I lived with my husband Jim and our daughters in suburban Atlanta. I knew I'd want to be checking in on him all the time. I also knew that my family didn't want him anywhere near them. In fact, Jim had formed his suspicions about Call's mental-health condition years ago when he'd first met him, even before Call had left us. And after Call returned, Jim didn't want him to be at our house because, well, who knew how he might act out?

"Call was pretty frightening from the perspective of just being on the edge," Jim recalls. "I never really knew what we were going to get with him. And that was a big concern of mine. I didn't want the kids around him alone. It just didn't happen."

No surprise, my daughters had their concerns, too. Like their father, they were suspicious before they'd even had a chance to see him after his return. (The last time Kim had met him, she was little, and Lauren had never seen him at all.) Who wants to invite an unstable person into their life? To me, he was the brother I'd always known, and I couldn't imagine him hurting anyone. Kim remembers, "It was difficult for all of us. He was just very foreign. He was in a daze. But we knew how important this was for you, Mom."

For his part, it turned out that Call wasn't comfortable moving to Atlanta. When I tried to suggest it, he didn't throw a fit, but he firmly said no.

Still, I wanted him back in our lives. I wanted him to have a chance to have a normal life. It was becoming apparent to me that he was seriously ill.

So, even if he couldn't live with us, it was my goal for Call to live in something like a normal social setting in a way that felt safe and nonthreatening for him. Eventually, I hoped he'd be able to live alone, be able to care for himself. The doctors and even Jim thought this was unrealistic. Their opinion was that Call would be more stable—and safer—in a group setting. As for me, I had no plan other than whatever specific treatment protocol we were following. He'd eventually go in and out of treatment facilities and his own apartments. But he was never homeless again.

After he returned to us, Call didn't share much information with me, but I did get a few facts from him about where he'd been. Then I did some phoning and some poking around to fill in the story—to get a sense of not only what treatment he might have received but also what we should try to do next for him.

When Call had shown up at Marge's to pick up her furniture, he'd been living at the Haven of Rest, a homeless shelter in nearby Anderson, South Carolina. He'd been there on and off for the previous six years. Although the facility wasn't set up to treat the mentally ill, the staff understood enough about his condition to have him seen by the psychiatric professionals at the local hospital. There, he received medication that they hoped would stabilize him enough to keep him living in the home.

Oddly, when I inquired at the shelter for him, at first they said they didn't have anyone named Call Richmond. Someone asked around, and the answer came back, "Oh, you mean Montana."

Call told me eventually that in his travels he'd lived for a time in Whitefish, Montana, which he seemed to think of as a second home. Eventually I guessed that he thought of Montana not only with fondness as a beautiful place where he once lived, but also as a kind of spiritual home, somewhere he'd been truly happy.

He wasn't having an easy time of it at the shelter. He was telling people there to stay away from his cows (as any "cattleman" from Montana might do), and he would sometimes brandish knives to back up his threats. In the short term, right after I met up with him, I hoped he could stay at the Haven of Rest a while longer. I begged the staff to keep him for a couple of weeks until I could find a place for him. But they were adamant that, because of his threats, he'd have to leave.

Our brother David drove over and picked him up. Call insisted he wanted to live in Greenville. David took him there and got him a room at the Salvation Army. But Call refused to stay put. He roamed around town. When I learned he'd gone astray, I drove from Atlanta to Greenville one afternoon and found him sleeping in the public library. He confessed to me that, after-hours when they'd lock him out of the library, he would sleep by a tree just a few feet away on the lawn.

David helped me convince Call that he should apply for public assistance and took him to the local Social Security office. There he filled out forms for Supplemental Security Income and Social

Security Disability Insurance payments for his food and shelter, along with Medicaid to help with his treatment plan.

Within a month, we had the Greenville Mental Health Clinic overseeing Call's care. He didn't yet qualify for residential care, so I told him to stay in a hotel I'd booked and not to go anywhere. "Please," I told him, "just stay here." I gave him some money, and I promised to stick by him and get him whatever help he needed, including a place to live where he could finally settle in.

Through this period, I was going back and forth to Atlanta to care for my own daughters, and my husband was traveling extensively on business. But even though Jim wasn't always by my side, I talked through the details of every decision with him.

One momentous decision Jim helped me make was to videotape my visits with Call. For as long as I can remember, I've had an eye for photography, and I had a video camera I'd use to record our family outings and celebrations. One of the earliest scenes I recorded of Call was right after he moved into an apartment we'd lined up for him in Greenville. That happened within a year of his return.

As you can see in the documentary, when I walked into Call's apartment once he'd settled in, there on the bed frame was the new mattress I'd bought him. The price tag was still hanging from the corner. The sight brought me to tears. How long had it been since he'd slept on a clean—I mean, truly clean and all his own—bed?

During this time, while Call was living alone at the apartment, we had the support of Greenville Mental Health. We'd just come back from a consultation there. "Call, we had some good meetings this morning, didn't we?" I asked him.

"We sure did, Rebecca. They're going to teach me about my hygiene, teach me to cook, teach me to clean up my apartment, teach me to turn the water on, even, Rebecca."

"And eventually you'll be able to, hopefully, just do it all on your own, without any assistance. That's right, Call?"

"Right, Rebecca."

It was gratifying for me—and it always felt like we were making such progress—when I'd take him on errands to the grocery store or the barber shop. When we entered Regency Barbers, I told him, "Call, you're going to look like a new person." He hadn't shaved his scraggly white beard in months. He looked like one of those drifters who make a few bucks during the holidays playing Santa Claus.

"I'll be so glad," he said, and I knew he meant it. He delighted in the attention.

As the barber ran the shears over his beard, she remarked, "You're a hairy fellow." And Call laughed.

"My eyebrows go every which way," he said.

As she removed the barber's cape, my brother turned to me with his close-cropped beard and neatly trimmed sideburns. "You look younger," I said, and it pleased him.

Bringing the hospital's social worker Cathy Gantt on board was a huge step in Call's progress. Cathy asked him about his money. She said, "Tell us what you spend it on during the week, besides your groceries." Call told us he'd walk to a restaurant near his apartment. And then there was also his favorite fast-food place, where he ordered what he called "lots of greasy stuff."

Cathy told him he needed to shower every day, wash his hair, and use deodorant and mouthwash. We were surprised to learn he didn't have a toothbrush or toothpaste. We got him those things.

I'd take Call on trips to the grocery store. He learned to select his staple items and pay for them, and he managed his spending money.

He said he remembered to trim his nails. Cathy checked his place to make sure he was keeping his things straight, vacuuming, cleaning the bathroom, and taking out the trash.

At the grocery store, Call made his selections, then he pulled a couple of twenties from his wallet—some of his weekly allowance—to pay the clerk. He waited for his change, and he counted it. These small victories seemed huge.

As Cathy noted, Call wasn't always careful about his personal hygiene—even after her instructions. But when he felt really good about himself, he would shower up. He'd always do that before Jim and I would take him to this steakhouse, his favorite spot to eat. You see, he had a crush on a waitress there. We were among her regular customers, and she made it a point to be kind to Call, treating him like any other customer.

It was 1999, and Call had been in his apartment almost a year. He was eating, taking his meds, and not wandering around aimlessly. He seemed respectful of Cathy's visits and advice, even though he never complied a hundred percent. But just when I thought things might start working out, my oldest daughter Kim suffered a major crisis. At first, Jim and I thought her problems had little to do with either Call's illness or my family's troubled history. We did understand that she'd felt stressed over my having to divide my time between our homelife in Atlanta and traveling frequently to check in on Call in Greenville. But as it turned out, we hadn't begun to appreciate how interconnected and snarled the events of the past, present, and future would become.

In her second year of college, Kim dropped in weight to seventy-five pounds. She looked emaciated.

Jim and I went to visit her at the University of Alabama. She bent over and her shirt rode up, and she was nothing but skin and bones. We thought she was going to die.

At the same time, I was dealing with my brother. I thought, "How do I make this work? I have to be there for both of them."

Jim and I brought Kim home from school, and we got her into therapy. We informed the university that she'd be on medical leave, but she never went back. We enrolled her in a residential treatment program in Atlanta that specialized in eating disorders.

Her younger sister Lauren was in high school then, and Lauren seemed relatively unscathed by the family's troubles. Like Kim, she often resented the times I was away from her while seeing Call and tending to the details of his care. A more immediate concern for Jim and for me was Lauren's judgment of Kim. Lauren has always had a keen mind and a sharp wit, and she didn't understand why Kim couldn't get it together. Kim was naturally upset that her sister wasn't more supportive. It was a dynamic that posed one more challenge for our family, but at the time Jim and I regarded it as fairly normal sibling rivalry. It was only later, when we learned the roots of Kim's suffering, that we all had to embrace forgiveness at another level.

To say that Kim had become obsessed with fitness during this challenging time is an understatement. In many ways, this inclination had come to her naturally. We're a sports-minded family. I'd been a bodybuilder in the 1980s. The physical training involved in bodybuilding was its own kind of therapy for me. I was proud of my body, and with the physical strength came reassurance and confidence. (Then I did one competition, and that was enough for me. I hated it!) Jim had been an Olympic-class runner in college. At his peak, he was ranked tenth in the world in the mile run and second in the 800-yard relay. So, when Kim took to running track and cross-country in high school, it was hardly a cause for concern. What we hadn't recognized was that Kim was using her exercise program as a way of repressing anxiety, along with a perpetual feeling of emptiness, no matter what shape she was in.

For a long time, her weight had not stabilized. After her first year of college, she had been a little heavy, but I wasn't particularly worried for her. Then, after that period of anorexia in her second year when we brought her home, she started binge eating. At her heaviest, she weighed 185 pounds.

It was during her therapy sessions that the truth began to come out. At first, it was disturbing. Then it was shocking.

Kim at her skinniest and at her heaviest.

With both Call and Kim in treatment facilities, I relied on Cathy to help take some of the responsibility for Call's routine care. We worked up a budget, and she helped me manage his expenses—rent, meals, cleaning service, and some left over so he'd have spending money.

It took us years to get Call diagnosed correctly. Some doctors said he had paranoid schizophrenia. Some said he was bipolar. We worried he was taking the wrong medications.

Meanwhile, Call chain-smoked, and at least he had a can full of sand on the walkway *outside* his apartment to accumulate all the cigarette butts. If he was forgetful about a burning cigarette, he could start a fire and not realize it until it was too late. That was a compelling reason not to put the butt can inside the place.

He also wasn't taking his blood-pressure medication because he said it made him dizzy.

But Cathy said, "He's diagnosed with major schizophrenia, and yet he functions fairly well."

Call's social worker Cathy said, "Sometimes Call listens to me, and sometimes he doesn't. Right?" Call answered, "That's right."

She noted, "Sometimes we do have to talk about what's healthy and not healthy to eat. And sometimes Call listens to me and sometimes he doesn't."

Call just cackled. He was a kid again, being a bad boy and getting away with it.

Call and I would spend several years seeing doctors for him as they tried different treatments and drugs for his mental challenges. The health professionals explored all kinds of therapies before Call could adapt to living in a group home. I was never sure whether setting him up in that apartment alone would be a lasting solution. Over time, I came to agree with his caregivers that, as a next step, the goal should be to get him stabilized and ready to move from the apartment into a group setting. One important aspect of treatment, after all, is socialization.

Although Call seemed to get along well enough with the people we'd meet on our walks, he wasn't about to go seeking anyone else's company—much less their friendship or their advice. It wasn't at all surprising that he would turn inward after so many years of being self-sufficient, however difficult it must have been at times. His fierce need to remain independent was also a factor. He was not atypical in this way. Many homeless people would rather freeze huddled in some doorway than seek the warmth of a shelter if it means becoming one of the herd. They refuse to be told when to sleep or eat, or when they can talk. And they won't be lectured to when they're not willing to talk at all.

It took almost a year after he came back to us before Call started talking to me about anything but the most basic caregiving questions. The exceptions were a few scattered, shared facts that I pieced together to get a sense of where he'd been. I already knew the early part of his story, the life he'd lived before he disappeared. Those memories were wounds we both had. Whereas I was badly hurt but pressed on, he was driven off the edge.

To understand what motivated him to leave and what wounds we'd both suffered, I relate some Richmond family history in the next chapter. I try to describe events more or less in the sequence in which they happened. But know that I wasn't fully aware of all the facts at the time the events were unfolding. Call didn't share important facts until long after he came back and I'd gained his confidence. And all during our childhoods, my parents hid things from both of us. There were also other painful memories I suppressed, only to recover them when I began to explore the past in my long talks with Call and then with other members of my family.

With some perspective on it all now, I see our family history as an intertwined network of troubled souls. And Call's disappearance was his way of acting out the pain we were experiencing in our own separate ways.

Chapter 3

The Richmond Family Legacy

Among the World War II generation, to all appearances, Mom and Dad were *the* couple. In high school in the early 1940s, Dad was the most handsome guy, a James Dean with dark curls. Mom was prettier than Sandra Dee, with a big, toothy smile framed in freshly applied, ruby-red lipstick.

I'm not sure whether my father knew Mother showed any signs of mental illness before he proposed to her. Soon after they were married in 1949, she had a serious episode. They were living in Atlanta. One day, Dad found her hiding in the attic. She told him she was seeing things. He got her admitted to a mental hospital. I'm not sure whether the doctors in those days knew enough about her illness or what to do about it. Apparently, she emerged from electroshock treatments acting outwardly as if there had never been a problem. However, she would continue to struggle with depression, and substance abuse as self-medication for her mental anguish, for the rest of her life.

When I look at photos of her as a young debutante, she seemed so happy then. Debutantes were real big here in the South. You had to be of a certain social set and status to be invited to the more exclusive dances. It's the old tradition of the cotillion. And then there's the legacy of the Southern bride. There's a picture in the newspaper of my father and mother on their wedding day at the First Presbyterian Church of Atlanta. He's in tails with a white tie and boutonniere, and she's in a dazzling white satin dress. The newspaper announcement, titled "Miss Mary Pennington Bride of Call Richmond," described every detail of that dress and more: "made along princess lines with the full skirt extending into a train. Her fingertip veil was attached to a coronet of seed pearls. Her only ornament was a strand of pearls."

Besides his good looks, my father carried the reputation of a brave soldier. My younger brother David remembers going up into our attic and looking through some old boxes that contained clippings and Dad's old Eisenhower Army jacket. He told me, "I realized that he was a war hero, and he'd done some pretty amazing things over in Germany." Among those clippings was a combat story, "Atlanta Sergeant's Action Annihilates Nazi Nest."

Dad had put his life on the line, he'd choked back fear, he'd faced horrors—and he never talked about it.

After my father and mother were married, they were so socially prominent that their parties made it into the local paper, which reported:

> Mary admits she's a little nervous, but Call can't understand why. "She's been practicing on me for two weeks," he says, "and she should be an expert cook by now—that is, with the menu she plans to serve Saturday."

Can you imagine? Talk about living in a fishbowl. But, to me, those too-cheerful stories never seemed to fit who Mom really was.

"Those clippings show a past and a side to my parents that I never knew," David said. "So it helps me put together some pieces to the kind of people that they were."

Call Richmond Sr. and Mary Pennington Richmond.
In those days, they were a socially prominent power couple.

Or that they pretended to be.

I have home movies of the newlyweds playing in the surf at Myrtle Beach. They look as happy as any couple ever. They hug and they kiss. There she is in her neatly bobbed hair with her prim one-piece bathing suit. Her lipstick looks perfect as she holds a cigarette above the breakers. Then there's another sequence, also at the beach, when she's hugely pregnant with Call Jr. Her hair is cropped close, but the huge smile hasn't changed.

My cousin Rick, the son of my mother's sister, described us this way: "The image of the family was one that was a very high social standing in the community. I mean, they were like the Cleavers. Call played football. David was on the baseball team. Rebecca popped gum, and I think she was a cheerleader.

"They were prominent people in Greenville. They lived in one of the nicest subdivisions in town. It was a great house to be around. People coming in and out all the time."

Even for a party at home, the men dressed up in ties and the women wore pearls. Uniformed help served them from an ornate punchbowl on a linen-covered table bedecked with fresh-cut flowers in cut-glass vases.

Social image was an important factor as we were growing up—what you looked like, what you wore, what you had. We'd go to these parties, laughing and putting up this front that everything was okay, that we were this perfect family—which we weren't.

There's a Kodachrome snapshot of us on a family outing, a picnic at our favorite spot, DeBordieu Colony, near Myrtle Beach in South Carolina. We called the place Deborah Doo. On this picnic, we were dressed up prim and proper. Did we go there straight from Sunday school? Mom is reclining in a lawn chair. She's dressed all in white, with a cotton short-sleeved blouse, pleated skirt, prim bonnet, earrings, and white gloves. Call Jr. was ten, in a blue suit, white shirt, and matching tie. Call Sr. was dressed exactly the same. There I was off to the side looking a lot like Mom in a skirt and blouse, but with no hat to cover my bangs, and in a white cardigan. I believe I was six. Baby David, not yet two, was on Dad's knee. We were all grinning our faces off.

I hate that picture. It was so *not* the truth about us.

To save appearances, we had a family rule of total secrecy. This lack of honesty just compounded Call's personal challenges. It's not that I can blame my parents so much. They were wrestling with their own demons. I'm sure they each suffered more than any of us could have appreciated as children.

My family at Deborah Doo. We dressed up prim and proper.

My mother's mental illness stressed my father so much that he was prone to fits of anger.

A related vivid memory that I must have suppressed for a long time came to me as an adult. I was just six or seven years old, lying on my own bed in the Pine Forest Road house in Atlanta. (This was before my family moved to Greenville.) Through the open doorway, I could see clearly across the hallway into my parents' bedroom. They were arguing again, and I'd been hearing them go at it for a while. It always troubled me to hear them, but it was not at all uncommon for them to argue.

However, this time it was different. Mother was sitting on the edge of the bed. Her belly was huge now—she was eight months pregnant with David. Dad was sitting on the other twin bed and facing her.

I sat up in my bed, and I watched in horror as my father kicked my mother in the stomach.

Why, oh why, would he want to hurt the baby? Why did Mother just sob and take it? Why didn't she run screaming from the room?

I knew that hadn't been the only time he'd hit her. His cruelty to her was another family secret. No one ever spoke about it.

My mother wasn't his only victim. He didn't *hit* me, but what he did left damage long after physical wounds would have healed.

Before I was in my teens, my father would sometimes creep into my bedroom at night. And he would fondle me. Like my mother, I didn't cry out, and I didn't run. He was the all-powerful master of the house, and none of us stood up to him. His abusive behavior toward me continued for years, acted out in different ways.

As with some other painful memories, these incidents of abuse were repressed, and I didn't recall them until many, many years later—after I'd been married and had children of my own.

But, as a child, I saw how my father often humiliated my mother. During my teens, I'd sometimes watched from the window as Mother walked down to the mailbox to retrieve her vodka bottle. Dad would put the bottle there hoping it would humiliate her. He thought having to carry the bottle back into the house in plain view of the neighbors would embarrass her enough to make her quit drinking. (Years later, after she was gone, he'd have his own drinking problem. He didn't drink daily to become numb and pass out, as Mother did.) Although I resented this controlled meanness he exercised over Mother, I understood why he did it. He was desperate to find a way to change her behavior, to get back the woman he'd married and the warmth they'd shared.

Even as I was growing up, I knew that my father was a bully, short-tempered and emotionally impotent. He'd experienced the worst side of human nature in the war, and he was never a person who could express his deepest feelings, especially his fears. Even though his married life had gone from blissful to distraught and disturbing, he continued to conduct himself in the business world with skill and careful calculation. He knew how to make money, and his children never lacked any material comforts. The responsibility weighed heavily on him, and he had no welcoming arms to come home to at night. He repressed his anger and his frustrations, and he acted out in a variety of abusive ways—violently to my mother, coldly unsupportive to Call, permissive of David, and inappropriately intimate with me.

And what was the nature of my mother's mental challenges? Well, for much of our childhood and to outward appearances, she seemed to cope most of the time. In my teenage years, however, I began to suspect that she suffered from delusions. Now I realize that, like Call, she was not able to deal with the voices and delusions, especially with so many obligations, secrets, and responsibilities at home. Mother kept up appearances while drinking to hide her pain and repress her fears. For years, she pretended to be happy, seeming healthier than she was for a long while.

One time, I was in the den and my mother was on the front porch. I remember her staying out there talking. I went out there and I asked, "Mom, who are you talking to?"

She said, "These people are talking to me."

I told her, "Mom, there's nobody talking to you."

She insisted, "Yes, they are."

That's when I realized that there was more going on than anyone had been willing to tell me.

Her admission form to the Marshall I. Pickens Mental Hospital in the Greenville Hospital System listed "hallucinations, unable to move," and "crying" as her symptoms and then added, "Voices told her that she was dying, even that she was already dead."

She was diagnosed with paranoid schizophrenia and underwent almost a hundred electroshock treatments.

After hearing me tell the story countless times—and living through the aftermath of Call's return—here's how Jim interprets those events:

> During the time she was drinking and taking prescription narcotics, I think your mom held Call closer to the family. That was his connection, if you will. It wasn't you, his sister. Clearly, it wasn't his younger brother. It wasn't the father. When she began to become more and more ill and more erratic in her own behavior, Call began to disengage from the rest of the family. The only relationship that he was left with was an abusive one with his father.

Indeed, there was always tension between Call and Dad. They argued all the time. And I remember when *I* ran away. I had my suitcase all packed. I just stayed away at a friend's house because I was scared. I remember Call coming and getting me. Nobody asked what was going on. It was just kept quiet.

By the late 1970s, Mother had attempted suicide twice and had been committed to the clinic four times.

When I was in my mid-teens, we were living on Chanticleer Drive in Greenville. I was in the kitchen with Mom, and she suddenly began shaking all over and fell to the floor. I was terrified, but I struggled to help her up. I strained to raise her. I was strong for my age, but my young body was frail compared with her dead weight. She'd gone limp, and my sense was that she was broken.

After I'd lifted her into a chair, I grabbed the phone with shaking hands to call my father at work. He came rushing home to take over. As soon as he saw her, Dad seemed to know exactly what had happened. He wrestled with her unresponsive body, as I had done, to get her into the car.

She'd had another nervous breakdown. I rode with him to take her to the psychiatric ward. She revived a little on the way. I remember her walking down the hallway, saying, "Don't let them take me. Don't let them take me."

From her medical records, I would later learn that she wrote to her psychiatrist: "I am in the end. I hear voices that are not real. I see things that look real that are not real. I am really going crazy. Please don't get mad at me and turn me away."

I still loved her very much, and I knew that she loved me.

Call's senior year in high school started in September 1969. His friend Rick Farnsworth recalled, "Call Richmond was an old good friend of mine. We played football. Call was a very laid-back guy, a little on the heavyset side. Friendly. Everybody liked Call. And since then, until recently, we hadn't been in touch at all."

Call's buddy Stan Johnson said that he and Call became best friends in high school. Stan said, "He was a very happy guy. He was a lot of fun, fun to be around. We just for some reason had a natural attraction to each other and kind of enjoyed hanging out—bemoaning that we didn't have dates. I remember when I'd go over to the house. I had this old car. I pulled up one day and came in to get Call. And Call said, with the straightest face, 'Stan, we would appreciate it if you would take the car and park it down the street. You're reducing the value of this house!'"

Stan remembered, "When Call graduated from high school, he began to show more and more signs of being a recluse—distant, even depressed. In many ways, I felt I was walking on eggshells around him."

In the early seventies, Call left home to attend Presbyterian College in Clinton, South Carolina. Not long afterward, he became withdrawn. This change in the behavior of a usually cheerful but quiet young man went largely unnoticed by our family. In hindsight, I can see that the uncertainty in our homelife, along with the intensity of our daily issues and problems, caused us all to miss or deny the clues to his disturbance.

When he was away at college, Call sent letters to us in Greenville. None of us picked up on the anguish he was expressing between the lines. Our father was so preoccupied with Mother's illness and his own fears that Call had to take a backseat, leaving my brother to manage somehow on his own. He didn't have any way to express himself. Without support, Call must have felt an overwhelming sense of frustration and despair. He was so sensitive. I felt he was picking up on my parents' emotions and absorbing all the chaos in the family.

During the time Call was attending Presbyterian College, I left to begin my first year in Columbia at the University of South Carolina. This is where I was to meet my future husband Jim. Not long after that—it was 1973—Call dropped out of school with one semester remaining. He moved to an old cabin in the woods outside of Greenville. Rick told us, "He lived in squalor almost in these old, run-down cabins." I remembered that, even when he'd been at home during this period, Call would never keep himself clean, as if he'd forgotten to bathe.

Apparently, he'd started having visions and hearing voices even when he was living with our family.

While all this was happening, our brother David was in high school, still living at home with our parents in Greenville. To avoid the tensions in the house, David would do anything not to be at home, just as I used to arrange sleepovers with my girlfriends. David immersed himself in extramural sports, then hung out with his friends for hours after practice.

Although Call had a bed in the family home, he wasn't around much, either. He spent a lot of time camping on the river and at a place called the Maranatha Retreat Center in Black Mountain. He bought a Toyota Land Cruiser and talked to his friends about how the movie *Deliverance* made him want to live in nature. For a while, he and a friend rented a small cabin in the hills of northern Greenville County. None of his living situations lasted. Every now and then, he'd show up back at home.

Thinking about the period just before Call's disappearance, David recalled, "He would share about the voices he was hearing. How he was afraid of those voices. We learned about the time he was standing out in the middle of the road, no clothes on. And he was about to head out to Montana (where he eventually *did* go). Or when he was standing in the kitchen with knives in his hands, and they had to bring in four or five cops to subdue him."

The central truth about Call—which we didn't learn until after he'd come back years later—was that he'd been hearing voices in his head for a long time. Sometimes they were friendly, nonthreatening ones, but at other times, he said, they were mean and aggressive. Call was not able to deal with those voices when he was living at home.

It was December 6, 1977. I was with Jim in Atlanta, and by that time we were married. On that day, Mother took a handful of pills and washed them down with vodka. Dad and David had been out of the house, attending David's basketball game at the high school. Call was staying over at his friend Stan's house.

During his long absence, Call was a drifter, hopping freight cars.

Dad found her lifeless body and phoned Call at Stan's. Call must have rushed home because I remember he told me he saw her body curled up on the floor in the hallway.

That was when Call felt he had to escape. He disappeared from Greenville just days after her death.

After he left home, Call started catching trains and hitting the road. To everyone who'd been close to him, he'd just disappeared. Over the next twenty years, he wandered the country, riding the rails, alternating between temporary lodgings and outright homelessness, and drifting in and out of sanity.

David said, "We had no idea where he was. And he did call, usually around the holidays—Thanksgiving or Christmas. 'Call, where've you been? How have you been?' It was always some fantastic story. Working down in Louisiana, offshore. Working on the Alaskan pipeline. Hopping trains from one state to another: Nevada, California, Michigan, Minnesota, Oregon, Wyoming, Florida—and Montana. I even remember one time when he said he was on a fishing boat in Alaska. Then he'd be gone again. And that was the pattern, for years."

Then, when we wouldn't hear from him, we did wonder if he was homeless—or worse.

Call's friend Rick said, "We thought Call Richmond was dead. That was passed around, and I think that's what everybody thought. Call Richmond has died in the streets of Atlanta."

In those rare phone calls I had from him, he was careful not to give specifics of his whereabouts. So I didn't know how to find him, didn't even know where to start. I didn't know which direction to turn. I just thought, *I can't give up. I cannot give up.*

During his time on the road, Call didn't take care of himself well at all. I believe he had no concern for his body other than to find food and shelter whenever he could. He found work along the way, often volunteering at missions or shelters for his room and board. When the less fearsome voices told him to go back to Greenville, he did. But that was usually for a brief check-in with Dad. Then, suddenly and silently, he would disappear again, given a small amount of money from Dad to help him survive. I knew nothing of those visits until weeks after he'd left the house.

I remember that once during the time I was searching for him, I received one of Call's high-school reunion invitations in the mail and opened it. To my horror, it said that Call was deceased, having died on the streets of Atlanta. (It was the same rumor Rick repeated.) I was furious. Why had someone written this? The rumor probably began when the reunion committee failed to get any replies from him. I'm certain that no one in our family thought he'd died. Perhaps, because everyone knew he'd become homeless, it was just a guess that he was no longer alive. That announcement caused me fits of sleeplessness, yet I never faltered in my strong belief that he was still alive—out there somewhere.

In some sense, Call lived a life true to himself. My brother did the best he could, although he rarely asked for anything from the family. He was detached from family and community, and for all practical purposes, he *was* dead to the world.

The brutal truth is that Mother was not spirited away. As I see it, she took her own life. We might think the overdose of prescription drugs was accidental, but she'd washed them down with alcohol. She lost consciousness, fell to the floor, and drowned in her own vomit. I suppose there remains the possibility that she hadn't decided to die. In those last years, it had been her habit to take more than the prescribed dosage and to drink at the same time. Putting herself into a stupor by overdosing was her way of coping with her demons. But I've come to believe this incident was a suicide.

In any case, her death pushed Call over the edge. Apparently, Rick and Stan, and probably what other friends he had, knew it at the time. His mother had died, and he'd left town. To his family, the connection was not as obvious. We were all stressed, but Mother's passing was just a crescendo in a chorus of hurt.

As Call opened up to me eventually, I understood that he and Mother not only had a deep emotional bond, but they also must have shared the same deranged experiences. I could never truly know what it was like to lose touch with reality, but I guess that Call and Mother recognized each other's afflictions, felt each other's pain. Not long after he'd begun hearing voices, Call realized that she'd been hearing them for years. And as I've mentioned, she'd

Mom carries toddler Call Jr. Years after he left home,
I learned they both suffered from schizophrenia.

been admitted to a mental institution and received electroshock treatments—over the years, culminating in many, many treatments.

Perhaps it was the fear that they'd do the same to him that drove Call away. The thought of being confined at home with Dad indefinitely would have been terrible enough. We'd all been on the receiving end of Dad's fits of anger. Now that Mother was gone, who knew how he would act out? It may have even been Call's devotion to Mother that had made him stay at home as long as he had.

The last thing Call wanted was to be confined in any way. When he came back, that fierce sense of independence in him hadn't diminished. It was part of his core personality and identity, a challenge I'd have to deal with continually as I sought ways for him to heal and to cope.

One time after he'd started to open up to me, Call said he had regrets. He was sorry he hadn't told me about a voice that had come to him just two weeks before Mother died. He said the voice told him, "I am going to have to take your mother away." Call insisted that he'd always felt guilty for not telling me about this.

After he told me, I hugged him for a long time, whispering that I totally forgave him. I said that maybe he'd been right to keep it from me. He must have thought he was protecting me, after all. My explanation seemed to reassure him.

Call's confiding in me about this after he returned just brought up more distress about everything that had happened way back then in those few days not long before Christmas. If he'd told me at the time, yes, it would have upset me deeply. But I had Jim. From our home in Georgia, it was a long drive back to the family and our grief in Greenville. Jim was my rock, and at that point I was trying to distance myself from the insanity back home.

If Call had told me about the voices before he disappeared, perhaps I'd have known how troubled he was. I might not have put much belief in the voice's dire prophesy about Mother, but maybe I'd have guessed how much its fulfillment would have scared him. I'd always suspected, as anyone might, that he'd been running away from the sudden shock of her death. I hadn't understood his deepest secret. In the twisted logic of his disturbed thoughts, somehow he held *himself* responsible for it all.

His waiting for so long to tell me about how the voices had warned him about Mother apparently wasn't because he didn't trust me or lacked confidence in himself. It was because he thought I wasn't ready to hear the truth. Or perhaps he felt guilty because he hadn't done anything to prevent her suicide and thought I would hold him responsible or be angry with him.

Indeed, there were all kinds of painful memories from our childhood that I'd suppressed. I wasn't ready to face those, either. In chapter 15, I relate how returning with Call and David to the house where we lived on Chanticleer Drive brought forth a flood of memories—especially about Dad and his own possible motivations for killing himself years after Mother was gone.

Even though my parents' suicides—the two events separated by so much time—didn't seem like cause and effect, I got to thinking about how their souls must have been bound up with each other. In those fairytale wedding pictures, they were a gorgeous couple. Their happiness was genuine, and you'd think they had all the social advantages and material wealth needed to overcome any misfortune.

CHAPTER 4

Jim and Me, a Movie Romance

CALL WAS THE CATALYST FOR THE MOVIE WE PUT TOGETHER from recording my years of visits and caregiving related to him—from trials and errors to setbacks and recoveries. We titled the documentary *A Sister's Call,* and it's won some awards. Perhaps you've already seen it. Then we decided to write this book because I wanted to say so much more.

Looking back now, I can see how it all unfolded. And I think about Marge saying it had all been "a plan from Upstairs."

On one of my visits, I asked Call if we could do a documentary about his life experiences. He said, "Sure, I would love to have a story told about my life." I remember walking away that day thinking to myself, "He was just waiting for me to ask. It was as though he knew this was going to happen."

The movie shows how Call and I—and eventually my whole family—overcame challenges as we grew closer emotionally. However, it doesn't explore the spiritual side of our relationships. So, this book not only tells the story you see on the screen, but it also delves into the more important lessons I got from learning to communicate with Call's sensitive and generous spirit.

My husband Jim has been my rock. When I worry, he tells me not to fret about problems I don't have yet!

There would not have been any video—nor would I have had the courage to follow through with making the movie—if it hadn't been for the steadfast faith of my husband Jim Schaper. I knew intuitively I should videotape the story, although I didn't know anything about actually making a movie. But because I had his unconditional support, I had faith and trust that it would all work out.

I've always had Jim's emotional support, and that says a lot. There were many times when he disagreed with me. At the moment, he may have been right—at least, logically so. But, as I've said, I'm the emotional one, and my love for Call and my faith in our bond always pulled me toward my brother.

Along the way, there has been the emotional—and even the spiritual—dimension of our marriage. It's easy to say—now that we've been together for so many years and through so many trials—that we're soul mates. But it didn't always seem so. In the beginning, I suppose it was a strong sense of compatibility. We knew we belonged together. As life threw us challenges, we began to understand how the bonds between us were evolving, transforming, and becoming deeper.

Jim and I met when we were in our late teens, at the University of South Carolina. He seemed different to me from all the other guys I'd met and dated. It wasn't necessarily a favorable impression. He was more reserved. He rarely acted on impulse. His approach was to observe, to consider, and only then, to act. At the time, as now, I followed my heart whenever and wherever it led.

Our life paths might have crossed before then, but they didn't. He was born outside New York City, and his family moved to Atlanta when he was six. My family was from Atlanta, but we moved to Greenville when I was eight. Was there perhaps a day when we were children in some park or on a playground and our eyes met? It's just possible. If they ever make a romantic comedy about the two of us, we'll suggest it as the "meet-cute" scene!

It was far from love at first sight. I had to learn to get past his calm exterior, to help him open up. He had to learn to trust that my intuition was right at least as often as his logic was. The bottom line is, Jim is a realist and I am an optimist. We've grown to appreciate how each complements the other, even if we don't always (I won't say *never*!) agree.

As we spent time together, Jim and I began to realize that we each grew up being the most responsible sibling in our own families. Being responsible comes with adulthood, but it's all the more important when you have children—and wards like Call. You could say that Jim and I are both caregivers, but we're not micromanagers. We're there—with the resources needed—when it counts.

When I'd come home from seeing Call, Jim and I would have long conversations about what to do next. Jim had sustained me through all those years I was searching frantically for my brother. Now that I'd found Call, it wasn't the end of the road. It was the beginning of our struggle to keep him in the world, in our world where the "normal people" are expected to cope.

Jim worried that caring for Call would stress me to the limit. By then we had two beautiful daughters, Kim and Lauren, and they deserved all the love and attention a mother could give.

Beyond his concern, one of the aspects Jim didn't appreciate at first was how much my mission with Call would challenge and transform *him*.

One time Jim said to me, "I always knew that you had a deep, spiritual connection with your brother. And I'm beginning to understand, at least I'm getting an inkling, why people come together in this life. It's really profound."

For Jim's part, he'd risen rapidly in the business world. He'd become the CEO of an international software company, and our family never lacked for material comforts. As a result, he was self-confident and decisive. When he was worried—worried for me—I knew to respect his opinions and his advice. When he was stressed about some business issue or personnel problem, I was his balancer. He said I always knew how to go to the heart of the matter.

"You amaze me, Rebecca," he said. "You have this need to right wrongs. Not just with your family, but I see it with our friends. You have this bravery about opening wounds. You want to heal people from the inside out. And, more often than not, it works."

"It amazes me," I told him, "that anything you put your mind to, you just make it happen."

"Oh, I can get things done," Jim replied. "But I don't have the drive to change people. If someone isn't a team player, well, they can't stay in the game. But you, you get results where I'd think nothing was possible. And you've mellowed me, I have to admit."

Yes, I had concentrated on making a home—a comfortable, protected place—for him and for our daughters. No one knew better than I did how much the balance in my life could be threatened by dealing with the brutality and unpredictability of Call's illness.

When Jim and I were first together, he hadn't known much about my childhood back in Greenville. It was only after Call came back and I revisited the past that I began to understand the extent of the illness that ran through our family. As I said, I didn't appreciate how much Mother must have suffered. I only knew how much Call and David and I suffered because of her erratic behavior.

"Your family appeared so perfect to the outer social world," Jim said. "But when all their problems were finally revealed, it infuriated me beyond words."

Time after time, Jim and I shared hours of insights about Call and the circumstances that drove him to run away. But even then, we didn't suspect how deep the tentacles of my family's demons would penetrate. There was much more yet to come. I can say now that the commitment Jim and I built gave us the strength and endurance to overcome it all.

As I mentioned, a good example of how Jim and I made decisions together is when we decided I'd videotape my visits with Call.

One of our favorite stress-relievers was spending time at the swimming pool in the backyard of our home in Atlanta. One warm day, Jim and I were lounging in our recliners, and we naturally began another of our soul-searching conversations.

I'm told that screenwriters have a formula for creating emotional scenes. They begin with a disagreement about an action and end with an argument about values. My emotional scenes with Jim often began with a discussion about what to do next for Call. There would be the decisions about treatment plans and his personal needs. We'd wonder about what some recent change in his behavior might mean, as well as what new needs it might indicate for Call's care.

Often, as you might expect, our discussion would turn to what more would be required of me. And what sacrifice of my time and our family life this new circumstance might bring.

This particular time by the pool, I wasn't trying to be defensive or manipulative, but I started to cry.

"Why am I *so* emotional?" I sobbed, but I wasn't really expecting an answer from Jim.

"It's like therapy, I guess," he said. "You can't hold it all in. You need to get it out. You have to tell your story. *His* story."

I don't remember who suggested it. Can it be we both had the same thought at the same time? We decided I should take our video camera with me on my next visit. I would start to film our story. It would be like those old photo scrapbooks that had jogged my memories about our life in Greenville. Having the video would not only give us a record of Call's treatment and his progress, but it might also help us plan as we tried to decide what would be best for him.

"I'm going to do this for Call," I told Jim.

He gave me one of his wry, knowing smiles. "No, Rebecca. It's for you. For you to heal."

"No, it's not all about me. Are you kidding?"

Jim helped me decide, with Call's permission, to videotape our visits. That's how we made our documentary, A Sister's Call.

It was to be, of course, all about me. All about *us.* And perhaps about you, too.

Once we started shooting video, Call and I became closer, so much more in sync. We made up as best we could for all those years he'd been gone. (In fact, he and I got so enthusiastic about the documentary that I hired filmmaker Senain Kheshgi and her crew to help capture the scenes. She worked with us from 2000 through 2006.)

All my adult life, it was so strange, and it bothered me that I could not remember Call from when I was little. It was as though he had been an invisible person in our family. I could not recall his being on any of our family vacations. I couldn't imagine him playing outside with David or me in our childhood days. Oddest of all, Call was notably absent from our family vacation photos. Even as a child, he must have drifted in and out of our house at various times. Now, I knew logically that he wasn't some ghost. Undeniably, he'd been a real person to me as well as to David. And now his presence—after I'd looked him in the face on so many occasions—seemed to me just as real when he *wasn't* standing beside me as those times when he was.

Thus began my exploration of the silent and long-standing agreements made—not between human beings who occasionally feel spiritual but between spiritual beings who have agreed to share a human experience.

CHAPTER 5

Call Opens Up to Me

WHEN I'D VISIT CALL, WE'D TAKE LONG WALKS. ONE TIME, I asked him, "How does it feel, being here by the railroad tracks?"

He coughed, repeatedly. It was that smoker's cough he had. I realize now that I'd literally asked him to cough up his demons. (Nothing is unimportant.)

"Well, I'm glad I don't do that anymore." He wasn't talking about smoking because he still smoked. No, he was talking about his wandering, telling me he'd given it up. This was a reassurance, about all he could give me at that point.

He seemed to open up most easily when he and I would take these walks. It was only later that I realized how ironic that was, how looking down those tracks must have had all kinds of associations for him, many of them desperate and fearsome. He shared with me that kids used to throw rocks at him and that there were times he slept in the cemetery with his head on a gravestone.

"It feels like I'm going back in time," Call said one day, out of the blue. And he led me to a place in the woods where he'd spent a couple of years before he decided to leave town. Happening on an encampment—just a pile of mattresses, tarps, and garbage—which

Call and I had long talks as we strolled along the railroad tracks. Going there brought up memories for him.

must have still been a flop for vagrants—he said, "This makes me feel like how in the world could I ever do that?"

One of the anonymous residents had spray-painted on a crumbling piece of a wall "Home Away from Home Shelter."

I was so utterly captivated by him. I just thought—and had I been the only one to think it?—*What an amazing man, my brother, the stranger.* I started taking all these pictures (on video). I captured little moments, here and there.

Those early conversations with him were typically short. It was like baby steps. If I forced it, I knew I was not going to be able to get him to open up.

For years, he'd slept in places like this, a "Home Away from Home Shelter."

One time when I visited, I had the camera ready and rolling when he opened the door. Far from cringing at the sight of the lens, his face lit up. "Hi, Becca! How ya doin'?"

"Give me a big smile!" I prompted unnecessarily.

The laugh lines were showing around his eyes, and his big grin exposed a wide gap of missing teeth. The rest were tobacco-stained, and I made a mental note then and there that he'd need a trip to the dentist sooner rather than later.

"You probably didn't think you'd have a camera in your face the minute you opened the door."

Or maybe he did. In that moment, he was as natural, as spontaneous, and as genuine as a virtuoso actor picking up his cue. In a flash, he was that giggling kid Call, the pal Stan adored, teasing him about parking his jalopy down the street. I loved my brother so, and in moments like that, I was sure I could get him back.

One day, I sat him down in front of the camera. He was freshly barbered. His sandy hair on top had been cropped close and neatly combed over. His bushy beard had been sheared with number-two clippers to conform to the round contours of his face. He was wearing a fresh, green golf shirt. His cheeks were rosy, and his eyes were bright.

After we switched on the camera, he looked lost for a moment. Then he had the presence of mind to adjust the lapel microphone that was clipped to the open collar of his shirt. He knew he was expected to say something.

"I'll never forget the time," he began, "I was going to Asheville. I'd been on the road about a year then." That was around 1978, when he would have been in his early twenties. (As should be obvious by now, Call's recollections jumped around in time.) "I was pretty tired. I went up on the bridge, and I turned around. And a voice came on, and he said… I forgot what he said." Call seemed to lose his train of thought. "I was going to tell you something."

He fussed, frustrated that the memory eluded him. Then he remembered, "He, uh, he said, 'If you go back under that bridge, you're through. You won't make it.' Voices told me that I was no good, that I was going to hell. If I didn't do certain things, they were going to burn me. So I didn't go back under the bridge. I kept on walking."

And when Call said he kept on walking, he didn't mean to the next railroad crossing. "I stayed on the road for about fifteen, sixteen more years."

Then I asked him, "Did you ever hear *good* voices?"

"No," he said. "No, I didn't." He seemed sure about it. Then, much later, he'd change that story. There was a good voice—a voice he called the *God voice*—and it told him to go home to check in with Dad from time to time.

David said, "I can't imagine having to live alone and live with those voices like that. Out in the woods? By yourself?" He shook his head. "How do you survive that?" Then he gave a baffled wave of the hand. "Somehow, somehow he did."

Another time, on a walk, Call confided, "It started out as I was kind of unsettled when I left Presbyterian College and I had to tell Dad. I wanted him to be proud of me, and it didn't look like he was going to be able to. He said, 'Okay,' and there was just the look on his face of disappointment. That really hurt. I wanted him to be proud of me. I wanted to be successful so he'd be proud of me. It didn't ever come about, and I think that's one of the things that caused the depression to set in."

Call was talking about his own depression, but he could have just as easily meant Dad's.

I've heard it said that the onset of depression can result not so much from the loss of happiness but from the loss of the *expectation* of happiness. Many well-adjusted people have trouble believing they can live "happily ever after." But losing the *possibility* of happiness, becoming convinced that you will never, ever be happy—that must be devastating.

I asked Call, "What made you decide to go on the road?"

"I had about five dollars left. So I walked to a mission, and they let me stay there. When I woke up the next morning at the mission, that's when I decided to hit the road. There was no other choice. I'd be homeless in Greenville, and I didn't want to do that."

"Why didn't you want to be homeless in Greenville, since it was your home?"

"I didn't want to be labeled as homeless. I didn't want to be embarrassed. I didn't want to admit to my mental illness."

Again, the Richmond family image. Social standing, turning in on itself.

Call would have good days and bad days. This admission of his about why he left was the first time since he disappeared that I felt like we were having a real conversation. I was blown away.

I've had so many people tell me, *Rebecca, he is what he is.* But, I'm sorry, I don't believe it.

Kim told me not to have high expectations. "This is the way it is," she said. "He is who he is. But you always wanted to take it to the next level, for him to be bigger and better than he was."

My brother David was more optimistic. He told me, "Since you've taken over and gotten involved with him, Call has improved. The main thing is that he's stayed in one place. He's got a roof over his head, and he's eating regularly. Just the basics of life—he can enjoy them now."

But even David added, "I don't know how much better he's going to get. You're always going to try to get him to do better. I don't know how much you've set the expectation that he will get better. If he doesn't, I hope you won't be disappointed."

Kim also insisted my expectations were too high. "You're gung-ho. You're fixated on how he's going to change. He's going to be perfect. Everything's going to be great now that you have him. He's going to be on proper medication. He's going to live this fulfilling life, and he's going to be able to do anything and everything anyone could ever ask of him. And that definitely hasn't been the case."

It had not been an easy battle with Call. There were times when he was just so stable, and I'd think, *Wow, we're on the road to recovery.* I'd see Call starting to become what seemed like normal to me, and then Cathy would phone me to say there was a fire in his kitchen. Another day, everything would seem to be going great, and he would be stable. Soon she'd say he was out sleeping in the woods.

A major issue with schizophrenia is the patient believing that their psychosis is reality. They think nothing is wrong, so they discontinue treatment.

Kim said, "I know you would spend hours in your car. You would go and visit him, sometimes twice a week. You knew everyone at the hotel you stayed at, everyone at the front desk, because you were there so frequently."

I was gone, and my family didn't see me as much as they'd wish. Lauren said, "And we didn't understand why. We wanted to tell you, Mom. You need to slow down. You can't fix Call."

I was doing everything I could think of to help him. Doctors and clinics and psychiatrists. Trying to get him on the right medication. Talking to other homeless people. Even introducing him to psychics.

One psychic told him, "Spirits are drawn to people who can see things. You can't just try to ignore them or tell them to go away."

Call's reply was "They see in their world, and I see in my world."

Then I'd get back in my car, and I'd drive back to Atlanta to see Kim, who was struggling. She, too, was seeing doctors and psychiatrists. I was making sure she was on the right nutrition plan. But she'd gotten in the habit of hoarding extra supplies. "Why do I have all this food here?" she'd ask. "Maybe to fill the void, I don't know."

Then I'd be back in my car to go see Call. I was just so torn between the two of them. But I knew both Call and Kim would get better. It was an internal struggle for me, but I wanted to do what needed to be done for each of them. That was it. Nothing was going to stop me from making sure they would both get well.

I marveled at Call, the complex person and the soul that lived in him. Over time, he and I had come to realize that removing hallucinations can dull all the senses. Coping is surviving, and, in the mental-health field, the goal is to maintain. But getting along is not necessarily living. And just what is living "fully" for a mentally ill person? Yes, my expectations for him were high—how else would it be possible to find out how high he could go?

I had provided support for him, but he also had gifts for me. And I learned:

What shines through comes at unexpected times, for him and for me. If you've ever supported a disturbed person through these kinds of challenges, you know what I mean.

For treating mental illness, as with many other conditions, one type of drug is not necessarily effective. Several medicines may have to be used in combination. This "cocktail" may give results, such as an even-tempered mood, but the mix and the dosages must be monitored and adjusted from time to time. That's because the brain is such a dynamic and ever-changing organ. And who knows what the *mind* is?

Call did his best to communicate his needs, expressing to his therapists and me what he was going through. Even with me, communication was never easy for him. Sometimes, he would seem alert but couldn't even describe what was happening in the room or what he'd done earlier that day. In some cases, he was prevented from speaking by shame for his behavior, particularly if it involved a lapse in personal hygiene. There were times when he was just too proud, and his independent spirit would assert itself. On other occasions, it was the medication causing these disconnects. I'd realize I was speaking to the veiled face of a drug rather than into the heart and soul of my brother. Encountering any of these barriers would cause a delay in his progress. His path forward wasn't always improvement. We experienced repeated setbacks in his motivation and his behavior. But we weathered them all as we drew strength from each other.

I came to listen to Call, not just with my ears, but also with all my senses and with my heart.

I came to trust an inner voice. No, I wasn't having hallucinations. It's a silent voice, that gut feeling we all know but maybe don't trust. When I began to take responsibility for Call's care, I called it intuition. A therapist might call it subconscious direction. Later, I had other names—and helpers and agents—for this extrasensory guidance.

One reason I was able to hold on to my faith in Call's ability to heal and my vision for his future was my growing belief that he was exceptional in his goodness and his spiritual generosity. As he and I had meandering conversations on my visits, I could feel a warm and gentle, yet powerful, aura about him. When he wasn't upset about his own practical failings or withdrawn into a drug-induced fog, he exuded peace and acceptance. He would walk into a place and people would always smile and speak to him. No matter how rugged he looked—and at times he looked like a tough customer—I could see strangers were usually not afraid of him. It was almost as though he was an old, wise soul. On some level, just about anywhere we went, it seemed that everyone felt and knew this.

I found I could pick up on his energy whenever I felt disgusted or angry in my life apart from him. It amazed me how Call never, ever complained. Despite our often having to tell him what to do and despite that fierce sense of independence of his, he never criticized or rebelled against me or anyone else.

When we were apart, such as when I'd return home to Georgia after visiting him for some days, I would suddenly feel his presence.

I'd pick up the phone right then and call him. There'd be times when he would call me. It didn't take us long to establish a routine. For the next dozen years or so, one of us would call the other every morning at eight. Call would say, "Becky, do you have your coffee?" We'd chat about this and that for about ten minutes. I knew he sensed what I was thinking in those moments, even on the rare days we missed having our talk. When I was worried about him, sometimes I would jump in the car on impulse and drive to Greenville to see him. I wanted him to know and trust that I loved him and would do everything in my power to make sure he was safe.

Call's spiritual presence with me evolved and transformed. Perhaps my greatest joy in writing this book lies in sharing with you how it unfolded and what Call's help—yes, his help—became for me and for my family.

Call and I shared a closeness that never left me. He became an accepted and even adored member of our family, especially by my daughters. We all sensed he was a wise man, but he remained a man of few words. He saw clearly into my soul. Even though he lived in South Carolina while we were living in Georgia, he was always connected to me telepathically. Eventually, my daughters felt his presence as well. I remember how he would pick up the phone and call me to ask about Kim when she was going through some exceptionally difficult times. He would call about Lauren, out of the blue, when her boyfriend was giving her grief. It was those seemingly random phone calls that made me think his abilities were extraordinary. Both of my daughters would take the initiative to call him when they were stressed about something. They told me how much better they felt after talking with him. He always seemed so tuned in, concerned, and intensely interested. He never offered advice, never gave his opinion. Yet his concern, in itself, was comforting and healing. What he conveyed to them was a sense of peace.

I came to believe that Call was spiritually awakened as a young adult—about the same time the demonic voices came upon him. Call told me he'd seen an angel. He said he was very young, lying on his bed alone in his room in Greenville. He said that this appearance was a sacred gift to him, one he never forgot. He held this vision as his own secret treasure, and it gave him strong feelings of being truly protected and loved by God throughout his life.

Then there was his talk of his "other family." That was a shocker. He talked of little Marguerite, how small she was, with pretty, long blonde hair. He described this other family to me in great detail, even what they wore and the things each person liked. The way he described their clothes made me think of Amish or Pennsylvania-Dutch people, austere and simple. He said, "You know Rebecca, I was there, too." I didn't assume it was a fantasy. I didn't disagree with him but gently pressed for more. I didn't get much—no location, no time frame, no experiences. For all I knew, they could have been imaginary. Or maybe some kind folks took him in for a while. Had he lived in their barn for years, earned a place at their dinner table by feeding chicks or slopping hogs? Or—dare we even think it?—with his heightened perception and his alternate realities, was he remembering a past life?

Even though he didn't offer much of the story, every time I asked him about these people, he was consistent about the details he gave, using the same names and descriptions. "I imagine they are still there," he said, although he wouldn't say where *there* was. "I would sure like to see them." I could tell he liked speaking of them. He always referred to them as his "other family" and insisted that he loved them very much.

Then it dawned on me—I'm not sure what he said to make me think this—that this memory of Marguerite was from a long time ago when Call was a child, perhaps when he said he'd seen the angel. Had he gone wandering from home even then—perhaps only for an afternoon—and found companionship with this little girl and a comfortable retreat in her house?

And I had another thought. Maybe Marguerite was the real child of a family that took Call in—in Whitefish, Montana! Although my intuition told me this could be the truth, Call would never confirm it. But every time I'd address him as "Montana," his eyes would light up and he'd let out his characteristic joyful cackle. It must have been some delightful memory he kept to himself.

I found I was able to see into my brother's soul in a way no one else could. I saw a quiet, shy person, full of compassion. Here was a man who had survived extreme circumstances, hardship, strange experiences, and adversities in his life without resentment or blame. Call appeared to be broken on the outside, yet, I wondered, was he really as broken within? I was sure he had a lot to say—but might be afraid or incapable of expressing it. He was fragile, and some part—but not the entirety—of his spirit was indeed broken.

When I came to this realization after several conversations with him, I decided I had to be his voice until he was able to find his own. He was depressed, surely. But he was also *re*-pressed. Perhaps he'd learned that describing his perceptions and his insights caused apprehension rather than wonder in other people. Not everyone would see a seer as wise. Now, I'm not saying that every idea he had was virtuous or worthy. I doubt he knew the difference, at times, between demented distortions of the world and special knowledge we might call visionary.

As we sat in the woods one day talking, Call said that he always went to the woods to find peace. It's a habit that we share. He told me that nature was his peaceful haven, the place he felt safe and closest to God. In nature, he said, no one could judge him. He did not feel different from others when he was there. This deepened my connection with him. Nature expands this safe, trusting feeling in me as well.

The emotional connection he felt in the woods made me think how similar we were in other ways. No, I didn't hear voices, and I could more than hold my own in the real world. However, we both experienced premonitions. We often had intuitions we kept to ourselves. These feelings were likely to occur at times just before deeply emotional or traumatic events. For example, we both felt we'd anticipated the deaths of each of our parents. I was sure that this feeling was more than wish fulfillment—the childish desire for the pain and anguish to go away. No, we both believed we knew, without being told, the hour of their passing from this world.

As time went on, I invited Call to visit our home in Atlanta. Jim and the girls gradually became more comfortable with him. From then on, Kim and Lauren—each in her own way—began to be more open and interested in him, trying to get to know and understand him as a personality, even as a wit. I never doubted that they wanted to like him, to trust him. They were curious about his life, his travels, and the world he'd inhabited—physically and spiritually. They came to recognize, individually and collectively, that they'd been judgmental, and they finally stepped back. In effect, they gave Call permission to be himself and—most important to him—to express himself around them. They came to love and enjoy being with him. Call loved them in return—as I know he was ready to do even before he'd met them.

There was a time—a period of sustained well-being—when he felt safe with us, and we with him. We felt it was a significant length of time. It felt like years, but it was a matter of months. You take joy as it comes.

It was beautiful while we had it. It didn't last.

CHAPTER 6

Kim's Struggle and Her Revelation

Our daughter Kim's struggle with self-image and eating disorders paralleled the difficult path I was on with Call. During the time he was gone, Call had seen Kim only once—when she was five-and-a-half—on that surprise visit he made to our family Christmas celebration in 1985. He'd never seen Lauren, who was born the following month.

So you'd think that Call's influence on Kim's life, to this point, was indirect and mostly unrelated to her eating disorder. Certainly, Kim was buffeted, as Lauren was, by the stresses I felt in dealing with his maintenance, including all kinds of discouragements and setbacks. But these problems didn't seem severe enough to send Kim into a steep downward spiral of anorexia.

Jim and I had pulled Kim out of school at the University of Alabama when we first learned of her sudden weight loss in 1999. We brought her back to Atlanta and got her into outpatient therapy, followed by a two-week stay at the Ridgeview Institute, a behavioral health clinic in Monroe, Georgia. There, she joined a group treatment program for eating disorders. She recovered enough to return to college the following year, but it wasn't long before she was back at Ridgeview, this time for severe depression along with managing her diet and her weight. From Ridgeview, she checked herself into a more intensive program at the Atlanta Center for Eating Disorders (ACE) for six months.

It wasn't until this critical point in Kim's therapy that she confided a secret that went to the core of her sense of self and turned out to be a key reason she felt so vulnerable and helpless.

I asked Kim to describe her journey in her own words:

I'll never forget coming home after my first year in college, and I had felt the effects of eating cookies, cakes, and pizza every night. I had gained the traditional "freshman fifteen," and I was desperate to lose weight. I remember joining a gym for the first time, and I really got into strength training. The trainer at the time had me completely change my diet, often consisting of chicken, broccoli, and, well, chicken.

So, for a while there, I became what I call a *restricter*—a dieter with a list of "safe foods" that included a whopping five things—chicken, fish, sweet potatoes, broccoli, and flaxseed. That was it. Maybe an apple here and there, and possibly a stick or two of artificial crabmeat because the caloric density is almost nil. I remember feeling happy about that, and I remember putting it on iceberg lettuce.

After I'd been on the diet, I went back to school. But then my parents intervened and took me out, and I went into treatment.

After a few months of living in this treatment center, I regained the weight that I had lost, and I couldn't figure out why I was still so unhappy. I felt disconnected from my body and quickly returned to my old restrictive behaviors. A year after my starvation period, I boomeranged to the other end of the scale. I became obese for my height and size, and for the life of me, I could not fill up. I needed food and constantly more of it. I often felt empty and alone without it. I even had my own refrigerator in the garage, aside from the large one already in the kitchen, to stash my extra food.

There were times I'd eat a normal meal, then come home and have another. I was so afraid to feel any sense of hunger. Even though I was overweight and committed to losing the pounds, when I would feel hunger, it brought back all the anxieties that drove the anorexia.

I remember leaving the grocery store, which was honestly a living torture chamber for me because it created an immense amount of fear. Why? Because I knew I had to walk in there and make choices—choices that felt so foreign to me, and I didn't have a clue where to start.

The store experience was overwhelming because, for once, it was entirely up to me to make all my choices about food. I didn't have a trainer or a therapist to dictate what I could and couldn't eat. I'd felt deprived for so long that I had the desire to grab everything as if I'd never be able to have those foods again.

My behavior was hardly consistent. For several months when I was in treatment, I was seeking the perfect meal. There is no such thing, but I saw it as my duty to find it. I would actually break down and cry when I thought I couldn't put together the food combinations I wanted. For example, I considered a perfect meal might be a piece of chicken with rice, broccoli, and yogurt. If somehow the yogurt side dish wasn't there by my plate, I grew anxious. The meal wasn't perfect, which gave me thoughts of failure.

One day, I was leaving the store heading to my outpatient program in Atlanta. I'd been in treatment for more than six months. The entire staff knew me by name, which made me feel special. The co-director of the facility really took to me, and I believe he felt my pain underneath all the compulsions that surrounded me.

I made a big admission then—I told him I had $400 worth of groceries in my car because I was afraid of running out. Mind you, it was dead heat in the summertime, so anything worth salvaging was short-lived. He asked that we go to my car together to see what all I had purchased. I felt embarrassed and apprehensive, but I still gathered my keys, and we walked out together. I opened my trunk, and he saw them—bags upon bags of nutrition bars, meat, crackers, cereals, ice cream, and frozen dinners. You name it, and it was probably there. And, of course, all the frozen stuff had thawed or melted.

"Okay," he said. "So, Kim, what all do we have here?" He tried to stay expressionless as he lifted items from the bags.

"I was so overwhelmed at the store, and didn't know what to buy, so I kinda grabbed it all."

"Let's talk about this," he said as he saw one of many boxes of crackers I had purchased. "Why did you need this one when you bought, let's see, four others?"

"I couldn't decide. I wanted them all, and there wasn't one that I could decide on. I'm not used to having so much food to choose from. I felt dazed and speechless when seeing all of the new options in front of me."

As I said, there was something about just being in a grocery store that freaked me out.

Then I started to cry. I felt so stuck, so fearful, so full of confusion, and completely helpless. He put his arm around me and promised everything was going to be okay.

When she was in treatment to get her diet and weight stabilized, Kim said about her hoard of extra supplies, "Why I have all this food out here, I really don't know."

He asked that we grab all the bags and bring them inside. I remember him asking why I had raw fish in the trunk when it was so hot out. I told him fish was one of my safe foods, so I had to get that in addition to something that I considered risky—like crackers, for example. He nodded and told me it was best I throw the fish away. I agreed.

When we walked into the facility with arms full of groceries, he told me to head to the kitchen. Then he looked at me and said, "Kim, you don't need food to feel safe. The only thing you need to feel safe is yourself." At that time, the statement didn't resonate with me, but now it makes me cry. I'm crying because I think how far I've come on my journey.

> I was no longer starving. I was binging. And even though I had support from my family, from him, and from all the people at the center, this cycle went on for years and throughout the course of my twenties. I was in and out of rehab eight times. I feel so sad for all the pain and suffering I caused my family and friends.

During this two-year series of professional counseling and treatments, Kim began to understand the sources of her pain. Jim and I thought her obsession with sports and fitness was easily explained—and nothing to be ashamed about. The fact that it had triggered the eating disorder was troubling, but no one in the family guessed why.

Her disorder was so tenacious that I began to think she'd inherited some brain chemistry from my mother. My brother Call was also its victim, and it's difficult to say whether his condition was worse than Mom's. His schizophrenia had been formally diagnosed, but, years ago, Mother's might not have been recognized for what it was. No doubt, her self-destructive self-medication with alcohol and pills was no remedy for her or for any of us.

Was the same mental disease hovering over Kim? Would she grow progressively worse, hear voices, lose touch with reality? I wondered whether behavior that is diagnosed as a form of mental disease might be a deeper, inner search for God or safety or understanding of personal sensitivities. Does the afflicted person crave spiritual gifts—even exceptional experiences? Could the behaviors and the seemingly false beliefs be defense mechanisms that allow a sensitive person to cope with unbearable circumstances? To cope with events in their lives that might otherwise destroy them completely?

No one knew—until Kim told us after therapy—that my father, Call Richmond Sr., had abused her when she was a child just as he had me. Like me, she had simply accepted it and told no one.

In therapy, Kim remembered that when she was ten, we were visiting my father and stayed at his house. He would slip into her bedroom at night, sit down next to her on the bed, and fondle her. Even after the initial revelation, she never gave me details about what my father did to her. I felt I shouldn't ask unless she wanted to tell me.

This newly revealed secret made me feel doubly ashamed—first because I'd never told anyone except Jim what my father had done to me and second because, after my mother was gone, we'd come to trust Dad. He'd settled into a second marriage, and from all outward appearances, he was once again a charming Southern gentleman.

I ended up telling both of my brothers, but only after my father passed away, about how I was abused. David was skeptical, but Call knew I was telling the truth. David wouldn't accept what had happened to me until, much later, he found out about Kim.

Jim found out about the abuse of our daughter shortly after I did, when Kim was in therapy. As I relate later, both of us were sick about it, and we blamed ourselves for not suspecting Dad's inclinations and doing more to protect her.

Helping Kim triumph over her eating disorder and depression brought our family together. For my part at least, supporting Call had made me more sensitive not only to my family's welfare but also to all of nature around me. Along the path ahead, I resolved to share those insights with Kim.

I know now—and, believe me, I fervently prayed—that Kim's condition was nothing like Call's. Hers was treatable, I was sure, and I also was sure she'd get to the other side of it.

CHAPTER 7

My Mission and My Family's Journey

SINCE CALL'S DISAPPEARANCE, I HAD ALWAYS BEEN COMMITTED to finding him, then helping him, then keeping him close. I never doubted this was my mission, although at times I feared it would be impossible to carry it out. My family wasn't always as committed as I was.

Kim's struggle helped me realize how her challenges, like Call's and like mine, were rooted in the Richmond family history. I began to think that there was within our family a contract made among souls. As family members, we are on separate paths, but we share a karmic journey. And we reinforce each other along the way. We've become stronger and more effective as a unit. We delight in our differences, and we rejoice in our strengths—in our ability to overcome, and even draw blessings from, life's reversals.

As I became closer to Call after his return, I also drew closer to Jim. On a practical level, I wanted my husband's concurrence on the next step of my plan—whether it was finding a social worker for Call or seeking a medical consultation to see if the combination of his drugs needed adjustment.

In the years right after Call's return, Jim had a full-time job and was often traveling. At home in Atlanta as well as going back and forth to Greenville, I coordinated with social workers on the details of Call's day-to-day care and the monitoring of his well-being.

My experience with Call made me increasingly attentive to the spiritual aspects of my life and the meaning of my mission. Our experience supporting Kim made me wonder about how individual life paths converge in what some might call *destiny* but increasingly seemed to me to be a set of soul contracts negotiated on some other plane of existence before we were ever here.

Jim's contract with the rest of us seems grounded in his talent for business. He has provided well, creating a highly protected, beautiful environment for us to feel safe and creative in, just as he has for the people who work for him. His mastery of enterprise generates enough wealth to allow us all to live happy, comfortable lives, along with having the confidence that we will always have enough not just to cope in the material world but to thrive.

Intuitively, I seem to know how to provide the peaceful beauty that Jim needs. I've created private places of seclusion from the outer world, both at home near Atlanta and at the beach house in South Carolina. In these retreats of ours, it's easy for him to enjoy his free time while he is learning to unwind. I say *learning* because, as many business executives can be, he's a results-driven type. Were it not for me, his blood pressure might be through the roof. More and more, now that he's retired, I see him wanting to make time to enjoy his life with me, wherever we happen to be. Also like business types you've met, he hasn't always been able to express his emotions. Now he wants to express his inner thoughts and his gentleness—traits that in a boss might be misinterpreted as indecisiveness or weakness. He wants to speak quietly, without fear of judgment. Both in Atlanta and at the beach, our homes are places of safety, seclusion, peace, solitude, and beauty.

At times, I heard Jim describe his executive work as being like that of a diamond cutter. Cutting through crisis situations demanded exacting decisions and precise execution. Now I see his priorities have shifted. These days, he's more inclined to speak his mind, and he cares less what people think. His lifework now may well be to hone and polish the jewel of his own inner wisdom. It is my prayer that he will do this by accepting and allowing other people to love, support, and do for him in the same ways he has done so adeptly for them. Perhaps his mission is not only to spiritually enrich his own journey but also to support us all as a family soul group in growing stronger and lighter together.

Jim and I are always trying to make sense of the sometimes horrific things our family has endured and grown through—extending back to my parents and their star-crossed romance. And with him as with me, it's always the process of finding balance, then moving forward. For example, when we first learned of Kim's anorexia, taking her out of school and bringing her home to Atlanta was a no-brainer. But what to do next?

My emotions were raging. My worst fears were flashing through my mind, especially at night. Yes, when she was living with us after we'd pulled her out of school, I went into her bedroom to check on her repeatedly because I worried she might not have the strength to take her next breath. Then terror shot through me like a jolt of electricity. Was she in the early stages of the twisted thing that beset Mother and Call?

And there, in the middle of the night, Jim's calm logic took over. "What we know is, she has an eating disorder. Let's help her deal with that."

"But what *if*—?"

His answer was "Don't try to solve a problem until you know you have it."

Then there was our decision to make the commitment of time and money to take what might have been a home movie and turn it into a professionally produced documentary. Over a period of years, I worked with filmmakers Senain Kheshgi, Kyle Tekiela, and their crews to capture the footage. Then Kyle assembled it all into a documentary movie and helped me decide to go to the effort of distributing it, including submitting it to film festivals and showing it to interested groups and at public-speaking engagements. I relied on Jim for his business expertise, particularly in reviewing the necessary contracts.

Next, there was our decision to underwrite the development and publication of this book. After we'd finished the documentary, I felt there was more to be told. I worked with my close friend Eda to develop my thoughts, and I engaged an editorial team to combine those recollections and musings with the story we told in the film.

All in all, we could have built another beach house for what we've spent—and that's not taking into account the investment of literally years of our lives.

Our first motivation was to provide a way for me to both immerse myself in the experience of helping Call and to find a literal focus for my concern, an activity that would have me doing more and worrying less. I'm sure this was the only expectation Jim had when I began to use the camera. The scenes I captured with Call did all this and more. I came to cherish those moments, fleeting as they were, when Call's glee, his wit, and his wisdom came through. It's all there on the screen for anyone to see, including families who face similar challenges and who will doubt at times that they can withstand the stress.

As Jim and I have shared our experiences with other families facing mental illness, we've come to realize that anyone who has gone through something like this craves healing. And not just for the afflicted person. It is also for the family itself, for the support network that encircles and cradles the primary sufferer. When we've seen evidence of healing and spiritual growth, I believe such benefits came from two basic commitments—*transparency* and *truth*. To me, transparency results from honesty in all things—as in Kim's fierce determination to confront problems squarely and head-on. And truth is needed because denial can suppress pain only temporarily, letting the problem fester and swell until it inevitably bursts. Certainly, denial is a defense mechanism—an understandable reaction. Lying to yourself might get you through a day, but it can't promote healing.

There's a balance to be struck. On one side is truth and self-awareness. On the other, compassion and forgiveness.

More than we ever dared, Jim and I—and now Kim and Lauren, as well—have learned to allow ourselves to be more human and more vulnerable, and to show ourselves to others that way. In our forthrightness, we find ourselves easier people to accept, trust, love, and understand. Fully sharing all we are, including the parts of our past from which our deepest fears arise, we present souls who are seeking transformation. As we share our heartaches and embarrassing moments, we can shift, even dissolve, some of the weight of our burdens. In sharing, we gain an inner freedom and enlightenment. Any reasons we had to hide our painful secrets no longer exist.

By putting our shame aside, we have restored our self-esteem.

CHAPTER **8**

Call's Treatment Plan

When Call was first diagnosed, the doctor put him on a drug called Haldol, which made Call feel tired, flat, and unmotivated. It was like I was talking to a drowsy zombie and not my brother. After a few years and very little progress, we knew we had to find something different.

In 2004, a new psychiatrist, Dr. Sheldon Cohen, asked Call, "What do you think about your diagnosis?"

"I don't think it's right," Call said. "I think I'm well."

"Do you think you're perfectly well?"

"That's up to you," Call said.

"I said do *you* think you're well."

"I think I am."

"Quite frankly, in reading the records, I can see why they were concerned about you," Dr. Cohen told Call. "Do you think these shrinks are crazy because they want to give you psychotropic medication?"

"That's what I was saying all along," Call explained. "I just lost my temper one time, and they sent me right over to Anderson Mental Health Clinic. They put me right under the wings of a psychiatrist there. They put me right on Haldol. Told me I had paranoid schizophrenia for doing that, and it wasn't even serious."

I told him, "You're going to feel things you never felt before, and I'm going to be right there with you." He smiled and said, "I know you will."

"I would say, after reading over the material, that you got some big-time problems, fella."

I heard the doctor say this to him, and it seemed an abrupt way of getting Call to face his denial. Call wasn't upset about it. He accepted what the man had to say. I don't think he was in denial, either. What I think Call was trying to say was that he was managing as well as anyone could expect of him.

I met with the doctor privately later. "You feel a strong obligation to try to help this brother of yours," he said to me. "Which is good, because without you, he isn't going to get very far. The best I could give you is that there's something missing in this fellow in terms of getting involved with life. Where does it come from? If he got medication, and I see this in a lot of people, if you're overmedicated, you just don't feel like doing much."

Dr. Cohen determined that Call was severely overmedicated with Haldol and prescribed a different treatment.

In describing the new course of treatment to Call, I told him, "You're going to feel things that you probably never felt before. And I'll be right there with you." The primary concern was that, along

I saw then that a light had turned on in Call. He was fully present in the moment. He was talkative at times, and he was witty.

with lucidity, those unwanted hallucinations and behaviors might revisit him occasionally.

"I know you will," he said.

From this point, I saw that a light had turned on in Call. He was fully present in the moment. He was more likely to seem to be in control of his own thoughts and actions. He was talkative at times, and he was witty. I bought him eyeglasses and dentures—a new set of teeth and a new smile. It seemed he started to live his life again.

This less oppressive treatment plan was a risk. But isn't living life to the full inherently risky—for any of us? A man is not necessarily wise who believes he's in total control.

As the years went by, Call and I bonded more deeply. The dimension was psychic, even supernatural. I learned to hear Call and sense him in ways I hadn't known when we were first reunited. Call's memories and insights made me begin to seek a deeper, richer, more spiritual meaning to our relationship. Being able to have what seemed like normal conversations with him also helped me reflect on all the experiences that our family had gone through. I began to search for answers to questions that had been gnawing at me for years.

Delving into these issues, I grew brave enough to find—and then to face—new insights. I began to accept that, in helping Call and Kim as I continued to support Jim and Lauren, I'd be helping myself. I'd be seeing into dimensions of my own soul, on a path to that ancient goal of enlightenment—*know thyself.*

At least as far back as the days of my mother's delusions, drugs, and drinking, the Richmond family had been fractured and dysfunctional. It was amazing that David and I had come through—seeming outwardly healthy but with deep, invisible scars. And even Call, afflicted as he was, was a gentle soul. When he was appropriately medicated, settled into a routine, and calm, he was a delight.

One insight I had that I carry with me now is the realization that painful memories of my childhood are rooted in shame. Perhaps I can generalize from what I've learned about psychology. Until a child reaches her teens, she doesn't judge her parents. She assumes that most if not all adults are wiser than she is, even if their actions seem unfair or odd to her. When a child experiences a distressing event, she blames herself first. She assumes she is somehow the cause. Her powerlessness to change the situation brings guilt and shame.

I may have been exceptional because, growing up, I never felt shame, nor did I assume I'd caused my parents' distress. I was both confused and angry about what was happening to all of us. A therapist might say I was blocking my emotions as self-defense. At the core of my being was not sadness but a sense of understanding and forgiveness.

True forgiveness—not only of my parents but also and most importantly of myself—is the only path I've found that leads to inner peace.

I was profoundly sorry for my mother's distress. I saw the pain in her eyes, as I know Call did. As for the harm that came to me, I never felt, as some victims do, that I deserved or encouraged the abuses my father inflicted on me.

True forgiveness—not only of my parents but also and most importantly of myself—is the only path I've found that leads to inner peace. With that peace came a sense of wholeness, along with the self-confidence to take the actions necessary to help restore wholeness to Call and to Kim.

For treating each of them, in different therapies recommended for their diseases, I had relied on the techniques and the tools of traditional medicine. In trying to find the strength to support them, I'd fallen back on my traditional religious upbringing. As effective as these modalities might seem in the practical world, I refused to be satisfied with results that were just palliative. For the most part, the medicines masked symptoms. In the right dosages, a handful of pills could make daily life tolerable. But there was no healing in these treatments. Similarly, remembering a Bible verse and speaking it out loud in the quiet of my bedroom could calm my nerves. Prayer, as I'd been taught to practice it, always made me feel better. At times, answers came—not as some voice from the burning bush (as Call might have heard)—but as new options, opportunities, and resolutions that presented themselves.

I persisted in seeking enduring strength rather than simple or temporary comforts. I began to explore alternative medicine, healing practices, and spiritual pathways.

My new sense of self told me I had to start with myself. My new sense of self-confidence told me that I was not the cause of my misfortunes.

Chapter 9

I See a Light

Like many families, we Schapers cherish the holidays. A family gathering is a milestone event. It may be joyous or contentious or a mixture of all the emotions in-between. There will be joy, especially if there are newborns to be welcomed or elders who are still with us. There may be heartache and disappointment, perhaps from unmet expectations. In particular, the children of yesteryear who are now adults will not enjoy being treated like children again by their aging parents, who will always see them as their children, no matter how much they mature.

And the meaning of the event in the history of the family might not be appreciated until years or even generations later.

Thanksgiving of 2005 was a momentous event for us, but not because of these kinds of family issues. No, it was simply because as we sailed through life, here was a becalmed day on otherwise stormy seas. This was the time—the very special time—when Call came to visit and everything seemed storybook perfect. After he'd reentered our lives eight years before, I may have underestimated the challenges. Despite repeated discouragements, I persisted in the hope that he could eventually make do. More than make do—lead something like a normal and happy life.

Kim was still in treatment for the eating disorder, but we were seeing progress, and she was able to join us at the table. Lauren was home, too, and she and her sister seemed to be getting along.

This holiday feast was the fulfillment of a dream.

I'd invited everyone to our home in Atlanta, and I planned and prepared almost as much as if it were a wedding reception. I cleaned and I decorated and I cooked. David and his family drove in from Memphis.

What made it special in my mind was welcoming Call, not only to our dinner table but also into the family circle. He was finally in a stable phase of his treatment plan. He'd been living alone in an apartment. He'd been taking his medication, a combination of several drugs that seemed to balance him. For the better part of a year, he'd been running his errands to the grocery store, walking to his local Wendy's for some of his meals, and coping generally. His social worker checked in on him from time to time, but he was, for the most part, an independent fellow. This had been my fond wish for him all along.

This time, there wasn't a debate in the Schaper household with misgivings about hosting Call. I didn't need to take time away from the family to drive up to Greenville to fetch him. We hit on the plan—which he eagerly approved—of sending him a round-trip Greyhound bus ticket. There was no nervousness about his staying under our roof because he informed me he'd prefer to have his own room in a hotel. The reason he gave was entirely practical—Call wanted to feel free to smoke as much as he pleased, and he knew I didn't want that in the house. Whether this was entirely his reason or he was concerned about our sensitivities, I don't know, even now. I do know that both riding the bus unaccompanied and having his very own room at the nearby hotel increased his sense

Call celebrated Thanksgiving with us, and it was a milestone event.

of independence and self-confidence. And he brought that mood with him into our home.

We all sat down to dinner at my house around the holiday table. Jim was at the head and there, opposite him at the other end—in the traditional place for the honored guest—was Call. He was dressed in a freshly laundered tee shirt and slacks, complete with socks and leather shoes. This was his way of dressing up from his usual wardrobe of not-so-fresh tee shirt, khaki shorts, and sandals. He'd run clippers over his beard to neaten it up, and he'd combed his hair. His cheeks were rosy, and it seemed he couldn't stop smiling. Every now and then he'd come out with his characteristic cackle, a sure sign he was enjoying himself.

David and his wife Shari brought their kids Andrew, Amanda, Allyson, and Alan. This wasn't the first time Call had met David's

Jim asked him, "Call, have you got enough food on that plate?"

children, but they'd grown a lot since the last time, and they'd never truly known him as "Uncle Call."

"I'm so thankful all of us are here together, and to share this," I said as I stood and we toasted with water, iced tea, and Coca-Cola. "And we're thankful that Call, you finally made it." I admit my speech wasn't original, but it was sincere. The look he gave me confirmed he felt and appreciated the emotion in my voice.

I had everyone serve themselves buffet-style, and Call piled it on with obvious enthusiasm. (With his new set of dentures, I think he was enjoying food more than ever.) He'd taken not just slabs of turkey but heaps of mashed potatoes, green beans, and cranberry sauce. Plus three dinner rolls. Jim teased him, "Call, have you got enough food on that plate?"

"I'd say so," he replied. But Call went back for seconds—a couple of times.

After the meal, Call and Kim engaged in horseplay like rambunctious ten-year-olds.

After the meal, he and Kim engaged in horseplay like rambunctious ten-year-olds as they fought over possession of a dish towel. Call cackled with delight.

Jim remarked later, "For a long time it was very awkward. Call looks different, he acts different. But over the years, he truly has just become part of our family. And if people are uncomfortable with that, or they don't like it, that's just too damn bad."

At the end of his visit, as I sent Call off to the bus station, we hugged outside my house. All I could think to say was "It was great seeing you," and he said, "Great seeing you." I thought I saw a tear in his eye. He hugged back, careful he didn't crush his still-burning cigarette into my back.

I was so choked up, all I could manage to say was "Love ya."

Even though I felt gratified and relieved that Call was doing so well, I wasn't naïve about his prospects, nor did I think it would be smooth sailing from there on. I might have thought the worst was over. Knowing what I know now, perhaps I'd have worried less.

Another time, we took Call to see Jim's mother Marge in Anderson, South Carolina, not far from Greenville—at the same house where he'd showed up on that errand from the Haven of Rest in 1977. She greeted Call, "Good to see ya. I'm glad you could come. I got that recliner in there all ready for you."

Later Marge confided, "When I saw Call, I thought, my goodness, there's the old Call. I probably embarrassed the heck out of him because I gave him a real big hug. Because I was glad to see him! I just thought how wonderful this is for Rebecca to have him back in the family again."

Despite the successful family celebrations, there remained the persistent question of those voices Call heard, just as Mother had. When his medication was adjusted properly, he might be less prone to hearing voices, but it was still a possibility. There had been times he'd followed the bad voices—not to do harm to others, but I heard he got arrested for taking his clothes off in a public area. And during his darkest moments, Call would talk to me about how depressed he was. Those mood swings could have coincided with his dosage levels and combination of drugs, which needed to be adjusted from time to time. There was never a guarantee that, having achieved some measure of stability, he'd be able to maintain it.

I did believe, even when he was hearing voices, that he could pull himself back into reality. He was a survivor and amazingly strong willed. But, then, he had this soft, compassionate side of him, as well.

I remember Call could energetically tap into me and also into my daughters. When I was with him, he could easily pick up my emotions. He often asked, out of the blue, "How's your patience, Becky?"

Thinking back on those family gatherings with Call, I realize that there are those moments of joy you want to freeze in time.

You think, *If only this could last forever.*

As to life on this physical plane, of course, it didn't. As to Call's later life, this was indeed a period of calm before the storm.

As to our spiritual lives, in a real sense, I do think that the joy of those days is still with us, will always be with us.

Chapter 10

Thinking About Mother's Anguish

I SUPPOSE, FROM THE STANDPOINT OF GENETICS, THE ISSUES MY family had with mental illness can be traced back to my mother. But without her, Call, myself, and David wouldn't have had life at all, so what's the point? Who knows how long those traits have been passed from one generation to another going back millennia? We could hardly say it was her fault—unless her fault was the decision to get married and have children. But at that stage, I'm not sure she was aware of her illness. And even if she had symptoms from time to time, back then there wasn't the understanding in the medical community that conditions such as depression stemmed from disorders of the brain that could be passed from mother to child.

If anything as time went on, I'm sure Mom blamed herself—not her heritage—for her chronic unhappiness. She probably felt she'd failed in some fundamental way, a feeling that would have only deepened her distress.

I'm not sure how much I blame my parents for all the guilt and dysfunction we endured. On the one hand, I look at my parents' situation, and I feel they did the best they could given the circumstances. On the other hand, I can't condone what my father did to

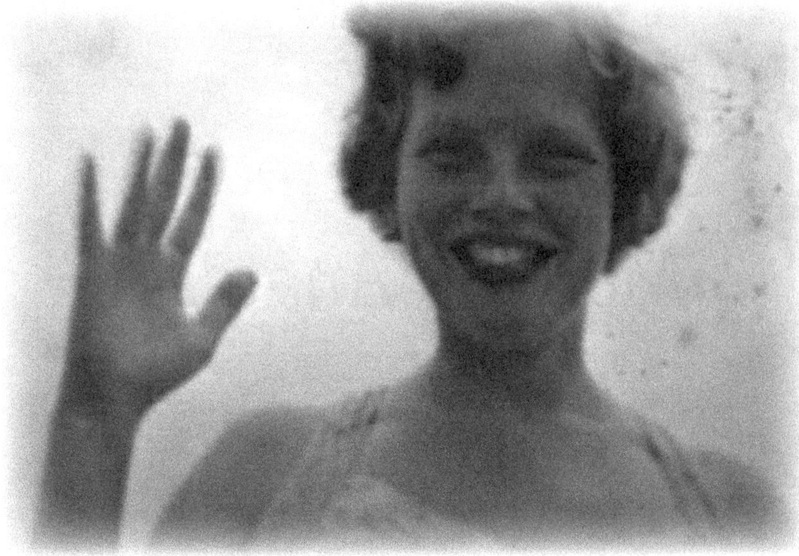

In those early years of her marriage, to all appearances, my mother was healthy, energetic, and happy.

me and to Kim. My father was at least as responsible as Mother was for all kinds of horrors visited on us. However, I don't think he'd harbored his demons from birth. The trauma he'd experienced in the war—combined with the stress of dealing with my mother's tormented daily existence—eventually drove him over the edge.

I was alive when Mary Pennington Richmond was happy, but I was a young child. The only way I can remember those times now is by looking at family photos and home movies as I grasp for fragments of memories. It seems like we always had a good time on our family vacations in DeBordieu with my mother's family. We're laughing and smiling in all the pictures.

There's an old Kodachrome print of us at the beach. It must have been one of those hot, muggy days. The sun was so bright we were squinting through our smiles. There was Mom in her

Here's my family on the beach at DeBordieu.
Note Mom's high-fashion hat!

one-piece swimsuit. She topped it off with a high-fashion bonnet that looked like a throwback to the antebellum South—with its full brim and a satin ribbon that she tied below her chin. At age twelve, Call looked proud and happy. He was starting to get his height, and his tummy was already bigger than his chest. Me, I was about six. Dad looked healthy and fit, and so did Mom. For all appearances, it was a picture of health, vitality, prosperity, and optimism.

It was around the same time, in 1967, that Mom would confide to her psychiatrist, "I feel so tight all the time, like I can't sit still. Help me."

It was also then—when I was six or seven—that I began to realize something wasn't right. I had to all of a sudden spend the night across the street at my friend's house. I was never told why. I remember my mother was gone for a couple of days. Soon I learned she was taking a lot of medications, and she was drinking. Then she was hospitalized after a nervous breakdown.

David was just a baby, but as he grew up, he witnessed her decline every day. "There were times in the kitchen when she had a bottle of vodka turned up. Just drinking it in front of us," he told me.

Oddly, it seems to me, David has fond memories of her affection for him. He wrote me:

> Rebecca, you ask if I felt fulfilled by her love. This is an interesting question because I think all children do feel fulfilled at the time, even in much worse cases, just because it is your mom. There is hardly any closer bond. As a young child, you don't generally have any other comparisons. So I think that I did feel fulfilled back then. I have always felt that Mom loved all of us despite the personal torment she was going through. I have such a mix of very different memories of her. I recall so well those tender times when she would rock me in the rocking chair in her bedroom. Do you remember it? The rocker had that soft, little squeak. Squeak, it went, as she rocked back, sometimes singing softly, "Hush Little Baby." She would get up with me, too, in the middle of the night when I was very young and had wet the sheets. She had a goofy buzzer that went off when she needed to come in to check on me.

David could not have been much older than an infant in those scenarios. I'm amazed he remembers anything. I suppose when the later memories are painful, perhaps we reach back, grasping for a glimmer of happiness among the myriad of childhood sensations.

It wasn't until I corresponded with David that he made me remember something touching. Along with all the distress and pain, our mother had a sense of humor. He reminded me:

> Do you remember that wig she wore? There were some funny times when she tried to make it look un-wig-like! There were those great times, too, when she and Aunt Julia would just be laughing together. I still have that photo we each have of her

> standing at the stove in the kitchen wearing that same bad wig —not looking like herself at all. Or—maybe that was her real self! She seemed like a different person to me then, someone other than my mother. I suppose that was my way of avoiding the reality of seeing her as actually being my mother in that all-too-familiar drugged condition.

As time went on and David entered high school, he says that Mother, in effect, was dead to him. And, I'm sure, as loved ones have to deal with the late stages of mental illness, they come to feel they've already lost the person they knew, perhaps years before the physical passing.

Call's friend Stan was a frequent visitor to the house, and his family also took Call in from time to time, giving him a respite from coping with our mother and feuding with our father. Stan remembered, "Everyone who talked to her knew that there was something wrong. You could see the anxiety in her face."

Anxiety—I suppose that was the "tightness" she expressed to the doctor. She was on edge all the time, continually uncomfortable in her own skin.

As I've already mentioned, Call carried guilt for years about having premonitions of Mom's death. One time when he was in a reflective mood, Call confided to the camera:

> The way she looked sometimes was heartbreaking. Nobody could help her. She wouldn't try to get any help. I'll never forget one time I was at the Winn Dixie on Augusta Road about two miles from the house. I got back in my truck with a load of groceries, and this voice told me, "I'm going to have to take your mother." In about another week, she committed suicide, and they called me at Stan's home. They told me she

> was dead, lying in the hallway. Isn't that something? That's really something. I don't know whether I ever told Rebecca that or not. So, in that way, I feel responsible.

Call acted as if somehow his not telling me about this at the time was an injury. Did he think that telling me—or anyone in the family—about the voice's warning would have prevented her from doing what she did? Without question, he wasn't at fault. How could Call imagine that he was to blame for anything? I don't think he would have dared tell anyone at the time—he wasn't yet admitting that he was hearing voices. But how must it have tormented him to carry that guilt around with him for so many years! The fact that he thought he'd done something wrong distressed me greatly.

In 2007, after Call's return and he'd been in treatment, it became clear to me that his illness was very similar to my mother's. I had this sense of déjà vu. I said to myself, *I don't want to lose my brother Call like I lost my mother.*

It was Call, in those lucid moments when he confided in me, who helped me fill in the gaps in my memories of our childhood. I had worried that I couldn't remember much about the stretches of time when he was not with the family. He told me that he'd go and he'd come back. It was only after Mother's death that he was gone for a long while. But even then, he had his ways of checking back, of finding out how we were doing, even if I wasn't aware of his presence.

A major revelation to me was that my mother had been ill much longer than any of us children had suspected. We eventually learned from the hospital records that she'd had three psychotic episodes over a period that spanned two decades. The first episode was right after the marriage when she told Dad she was seeing things. The second one happened right after Call was born in 1951. She had the third about ten years later. I would have been six or seven then, and it was around the time when David was born.

Reconstructing these facts made me wonder about the effects of postpartum depression on her. Was that condition something the doctors even understood back then? While the emotional trauma of giving birth might not have been the primary cause of her illness, it could have made it worse, much more difficult than it might have been for a healthier person.

I also realized that my memory of escaping from our home wasn't just a single event. Another time, when we were living on Pine Forest Drive in Atlanta, my father had me stay with the neighbors after Mother was admitted to a mental hospital. This would have been before Greenville, years before that time I saw her collapse. And it wasn't for just a couple of days. I was supposed to stay there until she "got better." And, yes, the time I'd remembered I'd run away, it was Call who came and brought me back home. What I didn't realize was that he hadn't been home, either. He'd taken refuge somewhere else, as he did until he just couldn't take it anymore and went off on his own journey.

It's been difficult reconstructing the events, sorting through the memories, and reconciling them with Call's own recollections and insights. It's difficult to align the memories—the images and the sensations—with specific periods of time. I tend to forget what age I was when an event occurred, and I seldom make allowances for the fact that I was only a child, without the ability or the experience to place it all in context.

Some memories stand out—as though suspended in time. For example, I remember vividly—and I'm sure it happened more than once—I'd enter the house or come from another room to find

Mother sitting demurely on a chair in our den. She was looking neat and pretty, all dressed up, perfectly groomed. As was proper for a lady, she was wearing pearls and heels.

She didn't necessarily have anywhere to go. She had taken the time and the care to look her best, perhaps in the faint hope that doing so would make her feel her best. She'd put on her painted, social face—a mask that hid her anguish. She'd smile at me, and I'd smile back. It wasn't like we could have had a conversation. I must have had homework to do.

One memory is incredibly vivid, and it's pegged to a specific date—two days after she died. Her funeral was held on December 8, a weekday, at the Thomas McAfee Funeral Home in Greenville. The turnout was huge, perhaps a hundred people. The outpouring of affection and sympathy amazed me. She was surprisingly well loved. Despite her illness, she'd made a profound impact on many of our friends and neighbors. They remembered her fondly. There must have been times when putting on that party dress and donning her mask worked for her—and somehow her innate sincerity and genuineness shone through.

Afterward the family received loads of hot dishes and staple food supplies at the reception at our house on Chanticleer Drive. One person after another—including many faces I didn't recognize—offered their condolences and asked if there was any way they could help.

David wrote to me, remembering it this way:

> What I do recall best is the funeral home visitation. All our friends and neighbors came to be with us, to pay last respects. There was such a long line of cars in the funeral procession, too. Mostly, I remember that so many of my high-school friends showed up to be with me. I seem to remember that the funeral was held on a weekday, so they had to be excused from

> classes in order to attend. Few things in my life have measured up to the appreciation I felt for my friends that day. Their presence was important to me. After all this time, I still have a special place in my heart for so many of my classmates who stuck close by me. Most of them didn't know what to say. Who would? Yet, they were there, and that meant the world to me.

In the weeks and months following the funeral, my father withdrew more and more. He was terribly sad, remaining isolated, falling into abject depression. I would call him long distance from Atlanta to talk with him, often several times a week. I remember how he would tell me repeatedly how overwhelmed he felt. He had no idea how to deal with his emotions. I hadn't had all that much experience with catastrophic loss, nor did I know what to do about it. After all, I was dealing with my own emotions. I was deeply sad too, trying to just cope. I remember telling him that he would feel better if he went outside to get some fresh air. I urged him to call his tennis partner, Ted Johnson. "Go start playing tennis again," I begged him. I felt he needed to get out of his head, and perhaps tennis could give him some focus. And it might release the tension in his body, help him move out of his depression. I knew this intuitively because I'd always been a runner. To me, exercise was always the best way to work through my feelings.

After the funeral, my father and David lived by themselves on Chanticleer. David remembered:

> After Mom died, it seemed to me that Dad and I were more roommates than father and son. He always came to my football and baseball games, staying involved with me in that way. But we had our own schedules. For the rest of my sophomore year, it was just Dad and me. Every Tuesday night was liver night because we both really liked liver and onions. I also recall

> feeling bad about going out with my buddies on the weekends. I would leave Dad alone, but he refused to have any of my guilt or pity. He always encouraged me to go out with my friends.
>
> I don't remember how much I missed Mom during high school. This may sound odd, but I was very much into being with my friends and playing sports. I do recall feeling bad that Mom could not be around for special events like proms, dances, and graduation. I think, though, that given her state of mind, I am not sure how many events she could have made even if she had been around.

Looking back, it's remarkable to me how well-adjusted David seems to be now, considering that he never knew a time when Mother wasn't fraught with symptoms—and considering how he bore the brunt of Dad's grief on a day-to-day basis after the funeral.

David summed it up for me:

> To me, Mom's death was a natural conclusion to her difficult life. This sounds like an obvious, rather insensitive statement. But what I mean is she was not herself for a long time for me. I have better memories of her when I was younger than I do from when I was older. She was so often out of it when she was medicated, drunk, or both. I know that this must sound harsh. It just seemed that way to me. But I don't ever remember being mad with Mom about any of her actions. I don't think she could help them. I knew in my heart that she was ill and that Dad was of little help to her. I also saw that she would be so much worse when he would yell at her. Yes, Mom's death, although hard for me at age fifteen, honestly, was somewhat of a relief for me. I knew she was no longer in all that pain.

That's David—practical and sensible. A good husband and father. And a resilient soul. He and Call bore much the same stresses, but what a difference in the paths their lives took!

There's one more remarkable aspect of Mother's character I should mention. Besides her ladylike composure, her fashion sense, her Southern manners, her occasional good humor, and her loving-kindness to her neighbors, she had another exemplary trait. She never gave up on her Christian faith.

I believe it has been that faith, that core belief, which led me eventually to a strong sense of my own spirituality. My viewpoint now is quite apart from anything like religious doctrine. If it was Mother's unshakable belief that inspired me, it was Call's example and compassion that led me the rest of the way. The direction of my journey was from coping with Call's mental illness to discovering my spiritual awakening. That has been my cosmic arc. That's my starry path.

The illness that my mother and Call shared is brutal and devastating. No one in this life would take it on if they had a choice. But as I've mentioned before, and it will take me the rest of this book to explore, I've come to appreciate—and, I think, some medical and spiritual practitioners agree—that schizophrenia, as with some other types of altered mental states, not only brings suffering but also exceptional talents. No one would wish for this horrific disease to gain its insights. Yet I have no doubt whatsoever that Call could see into my soul and that he was possessed—blessed with—with an extraordinary bounty of love. On occasion, in unguarded moments when he was relaxed, I could see it shine through. I saw the smile, I heard his characteristic cackle, and I knew he was enormously amused by life—and by his uncanny ability to survive its turmoil.

Existential philosophers say that life is fundamentally empty and meaningless. What's more, they say that's good news—because whatever meaning you do find, whatever belief you find useful, is valid. Some people might think that I discovered my spirituality as a way of finding meaning and value in traumatic experiences. That would be a pragmatic point of view. Perhaps David would agree (he's a devout Christian, by the way).

I don't see it that way. Yes, I discovered joy in my newfound relationship with Call. Difficult as it was piecing together the memories, I came to appreciate the gifts of affection and compassion my Mother bestowed on me, seemingly in spite of herself.

When I say that no one would choose schizophrenia to gain its gifts, I've come to believe that's true only on this plane of existence. I do think—no, I feel strongly—that immortal souls make precisely such choices and that they contract with other beings to act them out on Earth.

Like I say, it will take me the rest of the book to explain why I am so sure.

CHAPTER **11**

I Reflect on Abuse and Its Consequences

As I DUG DEEPER INTO MY CHILDHOOD, I BEGAN TO REALIZE that abuse is a thread that goes back generations in my family. It was the cause of what came after I was born and a symptom of what went before. Not least because of how the experience of dealing with Call's illness had mentored me, it took years for me to understand how abusive relationships are intertwined in the fabric of our family. Call's generosity of spirit helped me heal—in ways I will explain in the rest of this book.

I can't say I know everything about my mother, even now. Learning the medical details of Call's affliction as I was helping him made me appreciate what anguish the same disease must have caused in her. Reviewing her medical records after she was gone was an eye-opener, including the news about those scores of shock treatments. I haven't learned anything about her past to make me suspect that some history of abuse prior to her getting married somehow caused her schizophrenia.

That said, the emotional abuse my father heaped on her—much of it in apparent angry retaliation for the suffering her self-medication brought on him—could only have made her condition worse.

Add to this the stress of two other factors I hardly understood at all as I was growing up. First, in reconstructing the dates and events, as I've said, I learned she'd had at least three major psychotic episodes. And a second influence—how much she might have been aware of my father's abuse of me—will always remain a mystery. Was she aware of what went on—sometimes right in the bed beside her—when my father was sure she was dead to the world as he was taking cruel advantage of me?

I realize now it's possible—and this is shocking to even think about—that his taking me in their bed was another means of sick retribution. He could have led me to almost any room in the house. Why did he do it next to her if not to spite my mother for disappointing his happiness and thwarting his desires?

Oddly enough, the baby of our family, David, who was born in 1961, claims he was not abused sexually by our father. His age, being ten years younger than Call and seven years younger than me, might have helped shield him. In David's early childhood, perhaps Dad was preoccupied with abusing me. Later, when he was tired of me—or, more likely, when I was old enough to resist—perhaps David was old enough as well to understand that he had the right to fight back.

When I was being abused and even long afterward, I didn't give much thought to the fact that our father had already abused Call, as well. No doubt Call was abused physically and emotionally. At the very least, Dad was rough with him. If the abuse was also sexual, Call never told me so. I did suspect, increasingly after Call had returned to us, that he had deep emotional wounds. I

Me and my dad, taken around the time he began to molest me.

always assumed that the source of his pain and the trigger for his flight had been Mother's death. I knew that he and Dad argued continually, but again I attributed this to Call's protective feelings for her. Call rightly judged that she didn't deserve to be the brunt of our father's anger. If Mom ever had a hope of healing, it would be through compassion, which she never got from her husband. Perhaps Dad thought, in his self-righteous way, that he could bully her into submission and at least the appearance of sanity.

Today, I feel it was the shared pain of abuse that drew Call and me together in support and healing of each other. It was a powerful, underlying, subconscious bond. He and I never discussed this, but I felt it was recognized and acknowledged between us. I heard him. I felt him. I would find the best way to help him, as I wanted to be helped.

In my study of mental illness as I continued to support Call, I learned that sexual abuse triggers deep, lasting emotional responses in its victims. People who have been abused—whether in childhood or later in life—experience confused mental states, depression, and chronic anxiety. I'm sure his history of suffering caused Call to be in an almost constant state of anxiety. This fear could only add to his insecurity about his confused thoughts.

That's the practical, psychological explanation of what threw Call and me together after he came back. But on a spiritual level, I believe the soul contract between us pulled us onto the same path. This experience, this commitment to our mutual healing, eventually led me to inner peace and an awareness of our higher selves. I don't know what it was like for him. As much as I identified with Call and felt compassion for him, I can't presume to know his thoughts. I'm sure he was confused much of the time. Yet he had an almost unshakeable good humor, a composure that bespoke wisdom. Except for the times when he was in obvious inner torment, as when he went off his meds or the dosages were wrong, just being around him calmed me down.

One of the emotions that swirls around abuse is blame. Jim made it no secret, for example, how furious he was with my father and how unbearable it became for my husband to even be in the same room with Dad. But as with my mother, the causes of dysfunction and unhappiness in my father ran deep, farther back in time than we in the present can appreciate. It was only after my father was gone from this world that I learned he'd been abused by a scout leader when he was a boy. It was my Uncle Lea, his brother, who remembered that detail. I asked my uncle if he knew of other such abusive experiences in my father's life, but he couldn't offer anything specific. Then I had to consider my father's reaction to his war experiences, which today would undoubtedly be classified as post-traumatic stress syndrome. It would be as difficult for me to imagine what visions haunted him from the mayhem and butchery he'd seen—and participated in—as it would be for me to picture Call's hallucinations.

Those influences aside, consider also how deeply hurt my father must have been by the tragedy of his marriage. Call Sr. and Mary were the ideal couple—he handsome and charming, she beautiful and poised. They came from advantaged families, had an enviable home and lifestyle, and were socially prominent. Were any of her troubles apparent to either of them when they decided to get married? I have to believe there were symptoms or indications of stress in both of them, for different reasons, but perhaps the masks they wore for each other were just as effective in hiding their worries as the smiling faces they put on for friends.

How could you bear to see your wife's behavior deteriorate to the point where the only way she could cope was to spend her days in a drugged-up, drunken stupor? No more happy times. No more parties. No more sex. No more affection and intimacy. Not ever, from now on. What a prospect!

Meanwhile, he was fighting daily with his oldest boy, whose troubles had just begun to show. And he was taking out his frustrations on me in a misguided search for—what? Tenderness? Domination? Fortunately for David, Dad was mostly ignoring the baby of the family.

No matter how contentious the issues were within the family, my father did his utmost to preserve appearances. He loved preserving the memories of our good times in photos and videos. Looking back, I wonder if he was trying to convince himself that he was still the head of a happy, normal, wonderful family. Friends looking in saw our family only the way he wanted them to see it. Call Sr. tried to shield us from the outer world. Mother's situation was not a topic for discussion, and Dad made sure that she didn't meet anyone from outside when she was in a daze. Only we knew how deeply she suffered. In his own eyes, perhaps he imagined himself our protector. Amazingly, through it all, he did well to provide a substantial income and everything we needed materially.

I've hinted at the notion of *soul contracts,* and when it comes to reasons for our existence on this planet, my father's life story is incredibly perplexing. He was both hero and abuser, provider and tyrant. Then there are the added complexities of our *soul group* as a family. The inspiration for this chapter was all about how separate events in the history of abuse intersect and intertwine over the years, from one generation to the next.

What is this process but the performance of a contract?

Dad's actions seem genuinely evil, and yet even after I knew the truth, my heart went out to him. Kim told us how warm-hearted she thought he was, and she had just as much reason to feel betrayed by him. I feel that my dad's soul contract challenged him to provide, support, protect, and keep us all safe as best he could. Yet our soul group was left to pick up his botched part, completing it for him and for all of us. Yes, in my mind his contract was breached, and

Now I look back on Dad's photos and videos with different eyes. Here he is holding Lauren—whom he never molested.

he left it incomplete. In his soul's journey, he failed the responsibility of his real spiritual mission, even though he created all he set out to do in the material, social world. Now, I'm not sure what his mission was, but I suspect he wanted it to be more than just being a good provider.

Part of why this makes so much sense to me is because my dad never engaged himself in Mom's prayer group. He rarely went to church. I remember that he claimed to be an atheist whenever the subject came up. By the end of his days, without Mom or Millie, his second wife, he was left to face his inner self and his demons alone. He did not like living alone, and it's ironic that he had a Christian family from Greenville's Bob Jones University living with him at the end. They were a young couple with a new baby. They tried to help him all they could. The wife would read the Bible to him before he went to bed every night. Did Dad think this was a form of repentance for his horrific sins? His medical records indicate that he was in deep despair during his last months. His emotional state was fast declining. It's not so surprising that he committed suicide. He couldn't admit to me or anyone else the regret or the sense of guilt he must have had. His suicide note hinted at the emotion between the lines, even if there was no explicit confession. I'm not sure to this day whether he ever really felt regret. For me, it is no longer important what he felt. But his judgment of himself—which is what I believe we all must do when we get to the end of our earthly lives—would turn on whether he felt he'd betrayed his mission.

Now I look back at Dad's photos and videos with different eyes. I can see that although some were pleasant memories, others were clearly a violation of me. He captured certain expressions or movements that were particularly candid. Reexamining the photos he took of Kim, I wonder what was going on in his mind as he was clicking away. Why didn't I see those pictures this way before? I did not see most of his photos until after he died, and it's no wonder he never showed them to me.

Call said something chilling to me after we'd discussed Dad's photos one day. He said, "Rebecca, Dad kept a photograph of you under his bed." I was stunned. Nauseated. Violated, once again. I asked Call how he knew this. He said he saw Dad gazing at my picture in a frame. To this day, I wonder if Call was telling me the truth. I remember asking myself whether this might be a hallucination he was having. Yet I didn't see why Call would be making up something like that. I don't believe Call ever lied to me. Manipulation was not in his character. It was in his nature to be direct and sincere, no matter what the topic. And—something I appreciated only much later—the emotional content, if not the facts, of his hallucinations was not so different from reality.

Difficult as it is for me to think about even now, I can't get off the subject of abuse without relating it to Kim. I was sitting with her and her therapist when she told me. My heart sank. I felt like I was going to be sick. Honestly, I did not believe her at first. She'd been manipulative in the past. I wondered if this was just another attention-getting tactic. But as I listened, there was too much detail for it not to be real. I knew all at once that everything she was telling us was true. One part of me wanted desperately to reach out to her, to pull her to me and hold her, comfort her. Yet another part—perhaps my sense of guilt—made me freeze.

As I struggled to take in all she said, it was as if I were watching Kim from far away as she began to fall, plunging into a deep abyss. I knew that she had broken open. I wondered how I was ever going to deal with this horror. Abruptly, I shifted to fix-it mode. I thought I had fixed Call. I would get busy and fix Kim. I wanted to make it all better as soon as possible. Then maybe we could endure the hurt. I also realized that, in her breaking and her breakthrough, she needed to be right where she was in her treatment plan. I excused myself and left the room. It was so hard to go, leaving her there. As I got into my car, I felt something. Was it God's hand? I felt at peace. Suddenly, I knew for sure that Kim would get through this.

Fast-forward a few years. For Kim, it had been one scary, failed marriage later. She had been in and out of several therapy treatment centers by then. Even though I remained hopeful for her, I was still holding on to my own feelings of guilt. I asked myself over and over, *How could this have happened under my own eyes?* Never in my wildest dreams did I think my father could or would abuse my children.

Jim has expressed how the news upset him and how he wrestled with his anger toward my father and toward himself. What he didn't say was how angry he was with me. I wanted to know if Jim blamed me for Kim's abuse. I asked him, "You do, don't you?" He didn't answer, and his silence felt like a bucket of ice heaped on my head.

You could say my emerging belief in soul contracts is just a way of rationalizing my own experiences of loss and guilt. Take a snapshot of my life at the point when Kim broke down, and that could be a realistic assessment.

This isn't the end of my story, though. It's more like a beginning.

CHAPTER 12

Call's Process

ONE VISIT I MADE TO CALL BECAME PARTICULARLY meaningful for me. He had been in therapy for years, he was taking his meds, and he was living on his own. One day I drove up to see Call in Greenville because he'd phoned to say he had something to tell me.

I visited Call in his apartment, and he was eating a sandwich. Seeing him enjoying his food always felt like a good sign. He was recovering from a relapse, and his doctors were hopeful.

"I've been in process all my life," he said. "It's a white-shaped figurine on my right shoulder. I see it just occasionally, not very often." He showed me. "It touched my right shoulder here. And then it lapped over a little bit right here." Holding his hand above his shoulder about six inches he indicated, "It's about this high."

"What do you think it is?" I asked him.

"It's a process," he said. "It's a sign that I'm processed, that I'm in process, that it is a process."

He'd used this term *process* before. I was never quite sure what it meant to him.

"Can you help me out here? I'm sorry, I just..."

"Well, what can I say, Rebecca? A process is a process."

"Yeah, I know. But you're in a process to do what? I'm sorry, it's just my..."

I hoped to draw him out. The idea that he had a plan—any kind of plan—was a positive step. I didn't care whether it was fantasy or fact. I did care whether it would give him a reason to get up in the morning. If instead he'd been an alcoholic sworn to a new twelve-step program, I'd have said hooray.

"I told you," he said. "So that everybody can have a lot of wealth and be very wealthy. And the Lord God above can have unbounded wealth. And me, too."

"Okay, all right. So, everybody's in process to get their wealth?"

"I am. I'm the only one in it."

"God chose you to go in process, for you to start saving your money for the land?"

"Yes. There."

"Where is *there?*"

"Where He is, on the throne."

"Okay. You think God's trying to give you a sign for something else?"

"Could be. Could be."

"That maybe you're... reaching eternity?"

"Well, I don't know how close I am, but we'll just have to see about that." And he cackled.

Now, you and probably most of his caregivers might regard all this as simply the ravings of a lunatic.

Eventually, I didn't, and here's why.

I had no idea what this new plan meant to him. When I first heard it, I didn't know what to think about it. When someone really believes what they are saying, there may be no drug for that. In some way, I get it. You can call me crazy, but there was something special in his sincerity, in his commitment to this plan he had worked out

Call describes his "process." Was he describing his soul contract?

with his Creator. It was more than just his illness. That's what I've always loved about my brother—the sincerity of his commitment to his mission, even though he could never express in words how that mission would play out in the real world.

I didn't know how to interpret what Call had told me until a friend shared the following story.

My friend's grandmother had been prone to mini-strokes for years, but then she had a major episode. She was rushed to the hospital, was comatose for days, and then she regained consciousness. Clearly, she was not herself. She seemed to be in a perpetual fog. It didn't take long for the doctors to find out she'd lost some of her motor skills, as well. She couldn't get up and walk. Or at least she couldn't walk very far. And frail as she was at her advanced age, physical therapy was hardly an option.

She was in decline, and with the consent of her family, the hospital discharged her into an assisted living program in an extended care facility that catered to the mentally ill. (Her diagnosis was dementia—which is not the same as schizophrenia, but she needed highly attentive care.) She had a semi-private room. They'd get her up each morning, help her into a gown, and she'd spend her waking hours in a wheelchair. She got hot meals and occasional spins around the grounds on nice days so she could feel the sun on her face and get some fresh air. As far as anyone was concerned, it was just a matter of time before she expired. The family hoped her passing would be quiet and comfortable, and, if they were honest, they hoped it would be soon, considering the expense involved.

My friend lived some distance away and had not been present at the events or in the decisions that led up to his grandmother's admission to the clinic. When he finally managed to pay a visit, he met up with other family members who lived in the area and had been actively involved in her diagnosis and treatment plan.

It was a sunny afternoon, and they'd wheeled Grandma out on the veranda and encircled her with chairs so the family could sit with her. My friend found her smiling, with a peaceful look on her face as she basked in the attention of her children. What he found remarkable was that no one was talking directly to her. He assumed that they'd be trying to communicate, even as if to an infant. They seemed to ignore her. They chatted on about the news of their lives, almost as if she were deaf or had no understanding of language at all. They must have assumed she took comfort in their presence and that was all she could understand.

It had been more than a year since my friend had seen her. During that time, he had experimented with growing a beard, an idea he later gave up on.

When she caught sight of him, his grandmother grinned broadly and said—almost whispered so the others couldn't hear—"I like the beard."

Her comment unnerved him, not only because it seemed lucid and on-the-nose but also because it made him worry that she understood more of what was going on around her than she was letting on. Or perhaps she understood but couldn't express herself? Either way, he felt his relatives should be more respectful in their treatment of her.

What happened next was remarkable, but only in retrospect.

A light breeze had begun to blow, and my friend's aunt asked, "Grandma, where's your sweater?"

With a wave of her hand, the old woman replied, "I must have left it downtown."

My friend's uncle turned to him, and in a low voice confided with a chuckle, "She hasn't been anywhere but this place for a couple of months. Nowhere near downtown!"

Soon afterward, the party broke up. Grandma was wheeled back to her room, her guests bid her farewell, and they got in their separate cars to drive home. My friend stayed behind to wait for a cab to the airport.

As he was waiting, he stopped by the nurse's station and remembered to ask if they'd found a sweater. The duty nurse reached under the desk and pulled it out. "Sure, here it is. We wondered whose it was."

"I guess Grandma is kind of out of it," he told her as he took the sweater. "She said she left it downtown."

The nurse laughed. "That's right. They all call the hallways the 'freeway,' and my desk here at the hub is 'downtown.'"

The corridor with the busy wheelchair traffic was the freeway! These folks hadn't lost their awareness or their sense of humor!

In that incident, my friend realized that his grandmother was probably much more lucid than her loved ones gave her credit for.

When Call was lucid, I often thought he spoke in metaphor. Then, sometimes, he didn't say much at all, and just his presence was calming to me.

But she was beyond having her feelings hurt. She seemed amused by their inconsiderate treatment of her, the way a mother might forgive her bratty kids.

When my friend told me this story, we were commiserating about how little we seem to understand of altered mental states. I won't say "illness" because there was nothing dysfunctional about his grandmother's behavior. She was just expressing herself from a different viewpoint, as if in another language—at least, in a different vocabulary.

Soon after I heard this story, I thought back to my meeting with Call. Things began to fall into place. It might have been the biggest revelation of my life, but compared to the roar of anger over my father's misdeeds or screams of pain over the unfairness of tragic deaths, this insight came in like a toddler on velvet slippers.

What if Call was talking in metaphor—in symbols? What if he was expressing the absolute truth of his emotions and just not finding the right words?

What is a *process,* if not a *contract?*

What is *wealth* to an immortal soul, if not *joy?*

Who was Call bargaining with, if not his own immortal soul?

Chapter 13

Call's Symptoms Return

No sooner had Call made his new contract with God than he broke it. He'd been doing well for a few months, living in his apartment. He was taking his meds, and he seemed to be coping. After he'd been in various kinds of therapies for about eight years, Call plunged into a deep depression. And all his symptoms returned.

I knew things had gone wrong when I didn't hear from him for about a month. At first, I thought he'd gone quiet because he was doing well. He wouldn't return my calls. I hesitated about driving back up there because I knew how serious and proud he was about trying to manage on his own. Perhaps he needed some breathing room.

Finally, I called his primary social worker, Cathy. He'd broken off communication with her, as well. She'd paid him a visit and found him in a terrible state. There were feces on the wall and all over the rug. He'd gone off his treatment plan, and it was obvious he'd been drinking.

His landlords were threatening to evict him, and his social workers judged that Call was not living up to the Greenville hospital's mental-health rules—a condition of his treatment plan, which was under the clinic's supervision.

There were times I had no idea what to do with him.

When I saw his place, it was a total mess. Call started cleaning it up, and he promised in all kinds of ways that it wouldn't happen again.

I took his promises at face value, and I contacted his landlords. I begged them, "Please, just give us one more chance. One more chance!"

The owners had complained that the toilet was broken, and Call used it as an excuse for some of his misbehavior.

"How are you going to pay for that, Call?" I asked him. "Who do you call for your toilet?"

"I called a handyman."

"Did you tell them that?" I asked, meaning the landlords.

"No, I didn't."

"Maybe you should tell them that, so they know. I know you've tried."

Also on this visit, I took him back over to Greenville Hospital to make sure his prescriptions were up-to-date. His medical nurse yelled at him, "You have to take responsibility for your health. We can't read your mind. We don't know what's going on with you."

Call insisted his condition wasn't all that bad. "Well, I feel pretty good at the time. Without my medication."

"So, you just didn't want to take it?" I asked him.

"What usually happens to you when you run out of your medicines and you don't take them?" the nurse wanted to know.

"I feel pretty good." And he cackled.

"You're feeling good?" The nurse knew different.

"I feel pretty good. For a while, yeah."

"Okay, but then, long term, what happens?" she asked him.

"I start to hear voices. And I don't start feeling too good."

There wasn't much more for me to do. Call said he was going to take care of the apartment chores, and he'd take his meds. It appeared his landlords and his social workers would give him another chance.

I went back to Atlanta, and once again I was on the verge of giving up.

Kim remembers how frustrated I was. "You just threw your hands up. You were over it. You said, 'I don't know how I'm going to do this. I've exhausted everything into him. I've exhausted all my options. I've done anything and everything I can for him.

And he's just not reciprocating. He's just not getting better. I don't understand.'"

Thinking back on it, perhaps I shouldn't have blamed him for not trying. I had high expectations for him, and at times he'd come so close. But here he was backsliding, and I was exhausted emotionally.

I wasn't sure how much more I could do in this situation. In August of 2007, while I had Call's social worker monitoring him, I decided to catch my breath and take a trip to Europe. Kim had just come out of a treatment program at the Renfrew Center for Eating Disorders in Coconut Creek, Florida, and I was sure she'd love a change in scenery. We took Lauren with us. We girls saw the sights, drank some wine, and tried mightily to wear through the soles of our walking shoes.

When I got back from my travels, Call and I had another break in communication that lasted for a few weeks. Before I could get up to Greenville, Cathy called to say Call had been arrested and committed to Marshall I. Pickens Hospital, the same place that had treated Mother time and time again. According to the police report, voices in his head had told him to buy a gun and kill himself.

I called David, and he joined me there. He remembered, "Call took a turn for the worse. When I saw him, he was in an area they call 'the annex' where the more serious cases are, under heavy guard. He had been there for about three days. But then he was moved to a different area that's nicer. He became more stabilized."

Call explained, "I'm not going to blame it all on the medication. Most of it was me. I wanted to drink beer. I left a mess on the table I didn't clean up. I didn't really feel like cleaning it up. There were times I could have cleaned it up. I could have cleaned up my feces on the rug. I didn't. It wasn't the medication. I didn't, and

When Call was about to be evicted from his apartment, he couldn't explain why he seemed to have given up on taking care of himself.

I think that's one of the major reasons I couldn't go back there. I wasn't taking care of myself."

That time, he was in the hospital for almost six months. Then the doctors thought they had the medications and dosages right. There was nothing wrong with Call's treatment plan, they judged. He just wasn't following it. He had a behavior problem, and yet he was vowing to do better. There wasn't much more the hospital could do for him.

We had to figure out where he would go. Call was back on his meds, but he'd gained weight. His face looked puffy, his hair was mussed, and he looked exhausted.

That was the worst time for me, right then. Call had made promises—to God, even, in his so-called "process"—and he couldn't keep them. I worried that he'd lost the will to do better. And that's what discouraged me most.

I wanted to totally let go. I was at my end, and I felt I couldn't do it anymore.

So, as he was about to be discharged from Pickens, Call and I faced a huge problem.

He'd been thrown out of his apartment, and the medical team at the hospital thought they'd done all they could.

I was feeling little motivation to do anything for Call, but the responsibility was back on me to find him a place to live.

Around this time, I had to deal with another challenge. I'd come to rely on Senain Kheshgi and her film crew, who not only got us great footage and sound but also helped considerably with the logistics of my visits to Call. Senain had decided to move to California, and even though I wished her well, I felt abandoned. My thinking out loud about this with a friend led to a referral to Kyle Tekiela, who picked up the project from there and helped me carry it to completion as a movie six years later.

As I've said, it had been my goal since he returned to help Call achieve a stable lifestyle. I wanted him to seem normal to other people, even if he knew he was different. I felt eventually that he wouldn't be stressed about living in a social setting. He could make friends, run his errands, and greet his neighbors. In that way, perhaps other people would come to know him as I did. Perhaps they'd see the wise and humorous soul who was so dear to me.

I wanted other people to value him. Maybe no one would love him as deeply as I did or appreciate him as much. But they'd see him as a friend, as a warm-hearted, if colorful, member of their community.

My goal had been to help him gain the skills—and the motivation—to cope and to maintain. To live a satisfying life. To participate in love. I knew he was no stranger to love. I knew his heart was full of it. I was pretty sure that he was rarely confident to express it—except to anyone but me and to close family, and, even then, not all that often.

The practical question for me at this point was: *How should I respond?* I know my inclination was to give and keep on giving—to be there whenever Call needed me, no matter what the reason. To stand by him even if he was the cause of his anguish, even when he'd given up on himself. Even when it seemed to everyone around me that he didn't deserve my attention.

What about his caregivers? Where did their responsibility begin and end? At a minimum, there are standards of medical practice and ethics. There are legal and practical definitions. But these helpers are also human beings who had built up their hopes for him, affection for him, and attachment to him. What should their role be when it seemed he'd given up on them? When he'd rejected or ignored their advice, their prescriptions, and their helping hands? There are drugs to prevent hallucinations, but there's no quick fix for a patient who earnestly believes something that isn't true. There are pills to mellow angry moods or ease pain, but none come with a guarantee that you will want to get up in the morning, keep yourself clean, and put nutritious food in your stomach.

And then there's the deeper insight I'd begun to have about soul contracts. Now that my father was gone, it was obvious that he'd failed in his mission in significant ways. He'd provided for us, but he'd wounded us deeply, as well.

I suppose what worried me most now, when Call lapsed into another time of deep depression and dysfunction, was that he'd never achieve whatever it was he came into this life to do.

There must be souls who can't manage to stay in the light. Perhaps no amount of human effort was going to save Call from the dark side of himself.

But before I could help Call further, fate literally knocked me over.

Chapter 14

Dealing with My Overwhelm

At this point in my story, I'm going to back away from Call for a bit. He was still at Pickens, about to be discharged, and the question of where he would make his future home hadn't been settled. He was still wrestling with his issues, but Cathy was keeping an eye on him. As for me, I needed a break.

Be careful what you ask for!

After Call's last reversal, I felt so overwhelmed. After he'd shown so much progress, it was discouraging and hurtful that he seemed to have given up. I felt frustrated and angry. By turns, I blamed the doctors, the caregivers, my family, anyone who cut me off in traffic, and myself.

I couldn't blame *him*. How could I? Yes, he'd deliberately not taken his meds. Yet I was amazed that he'd been able to muster so much self-control for so long. That's what had driven my expectations so much higher. I really thought he'd be able to manage by himself someday.

But then, this.

I believe that when you're angry, when you are truly angry, you are angry mainly with yourself. Your anger arises from your deep-seated fear that you—and only you—are to blame and that you are as flawed as your worst fears and your unthinking abusers say you are. In the case of Call's illness, my deepest fear was that I had been wrong, that it was beyond his ability to get better and stay that way, and that I was wasting my time and needlessly stressing my family by taking on this impossible mission to "save" him.

The logical enemy was the disease, some bad pieces of DNA we got from our parents. But you can't be mad at a disease. It has no face, and it reacts not at all to your yelling or your tears. It's natural to take it out on the people closest to you—especially on yourself.

Abusing my family was not an option for me, although I'd had ample models for doing so in both of my parents. As I had done when I was a teenager living with them, I would sometimes leave the house rather than deal with the strife in Atlanta or at our beach home. Call's solution when we were young had been to run away and not come back. Back in those days, I'd arrange sleepovers with my girlfriends to avoid going home.

In my later life, I used to run as my way to escape, to get away. I'd put on my shorts, my tank top, and my jogging shoes. And I'd take off.

I ran to the point I abused the running—and myself.

Jim recalls, "Your running was obsessive. It was constant. There were a lot of times when our lives were wrapped around your ability to get a workout in."

I wasn't just running away from stress. I was running *toward* something, *into* something. Toward a sense of solitude and self-discovery, into nature.

Perhaps seeking solace in my alone time in nature was an excuse I gave myself. But my desire to be out there was genuine. I'd always been an outdoor person. I've always been happiest walking in parks, jogging along woodland paths, or running along the edge

When I felt overwhelmed, I'd go on long runs as if I were running away from it all.

of the ocean. In the early mornings or just before sunset, when I'm not moving among the trees or hearing the surf, I want to sit outside and meditate.

Our home in suburban Atlanta is in a lush woodland setting in a quiet gated community. Nature is just a few steps from the house. The trees are full of songbirds, and deer come to graze. But when I'm there, my responsibilities are also only a few steps away. Finding time to relax can be difficult, and although at times I might be alone, often I can't find any peace in my solitude when I'm in Atlanta.

We have a second home at the beach in South Carolina. There I find my true sanctuary. As I meditate, I'm rocked gently by the sound of the waves, and I can run for hours along the edge of the surf.

I needed it so much the running became like a drug to me. Even on family vacations, I had to take time to break away.

Even though at times it was a thrill and a comfort, eventually I had to admit I was running from my responsibilities. I was running from taking care of Call and from whatever was going on with my two daughters.

As tensions grew at home, I found myself going out more and enjoying it less. I knew in my heart it was time for me to slow down. I prayed about it. And I said, "God, help me."

I suppose you could say what came next was an answer to prayer. But it came with a lot of pain. It was a turning point, in many ways.

The event itself was hardly an answer to prayer. But it marked the beginning of a whole series of blessings. Now, we had a lot going on (when *don't* we?). In addition to all the usual family responsibilities, I was coping with two more stressful situations. First, Jim was preparing for an extended business trip to Europe. He'd be going alone, and I suppose my practical concerns about the household were compounded by simple anxiety about our separation. Then, just days before he was to leave, we'd been invited to attend the classic rivalry football game between the University of South Carolina and the University of Tennessee. Jim and I had been asked to sit in the athletic director's private box, and we'd eagerly said yes.

It seemed so hectic when Jim was packing for two trips—to Columbia for football and then to Europe—while I was trying to think through all the things I wanted to do to support him. We loaded up the trunk of our car and drove for three hours to a hotel in Columbia, where it would be a home game for USC.

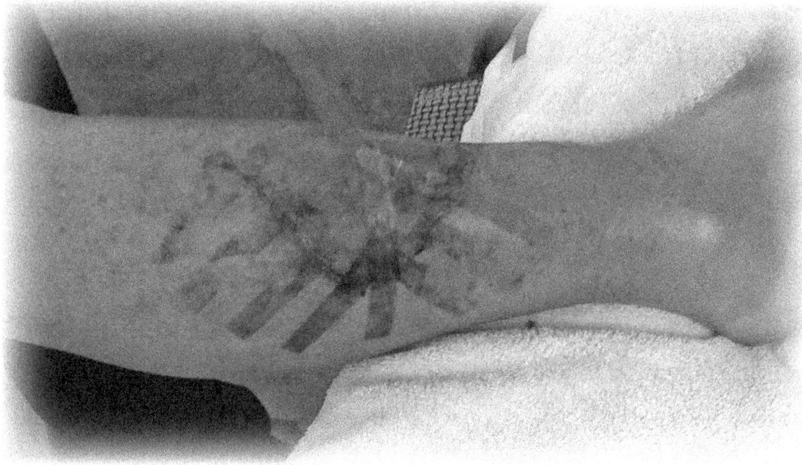

My accident with the moped left this huge gash in my leg.

It was a crisp morning in late October of 2008, the day of the big game. I set out from the hotel for a run. I ran for a couple of miles, and it helped clear my head, although I was still fretting about Jim's leaving. I was running along the shoulder of the road. I was looking one way for oncoming traffic when I was struck from the other direction. The rider of the moped must not have seen me either. The metal tore into my calf and made a huge gash in my flesh.

The rider was thrown from his bike, so he was injured as well. Another man saw it all and rushed over. I used his cell phone to call Jim, but he didn't pick up! He didn't recognize the number. After two more tries, I got through to him.

The rider and I rode in the same ambulance to the hospital. That felt awkward. Jim met me in the emergency room. Of course, we didn't make it to the game, and it was the athletic director himself who got me referred to the doctor who fixed me up.

I knew when the moped hit me that it would be a while before I'd be running again. I hadn't known how to ask for help with what was almost an addiction. I hadn't any idea what I wanted God to do for me.

Then the ugly wound I suffered brought me relief. And, after that, everything changed.

Jim goes so far as to say that our souls became one because of the accident. As he explained it, "It wasn't because we were a hundred percent aligned but because we weren't. I was set to give that series of speeches in Europe. It was a big deal, and, after all, I was the head of the company. Although your injury was serious enough, it wasn't life-threatening. And I wouldn't have been gone long. So I think you assumed I'd go anyway."

But he didn't, and it was a turning point in our relationship.

It wasn't that we weren't getting along. The stress with Call had made me preoccupied at times, and we were all irritable from time to time.

Then Jim gave me the gift of his staying home, and I gave him back my gratitude. Does it make sense to say that I made him the gift of my pain? To our friends and his business associates, perhaps the event didn't seem all that momentous. It quickly became apparent that I wouldn't be crippled, and the surgery was much less involved than a major operation would have been. Don't people voluntarily submit to even riskier outpatient procedures every day?

As Jim said:

> You talked constantly about your responsibilities. You were committed to nurturing me and our daughters. And you'd taken on this seemingly impossible mission with Call. But, you see, I had my business responsibilities, and I took them every bit as seriously. People's jobs and the welfare of their families depended on my decisions. The whole company looked to my leadership, and then there were our customers who came to us

> because they had critical business needs that had to be solved. But I canceled my trip and I stayed behind. It was because, for the first time in our marriage, I realized you were more important to me than any of that. And I suppose I sensed how much you needed, not just physical healing, but my emotional support. Perhaps I didn't appreciate it fully when it happened, but that accident was a life-changer. I feared you'd be disfigured. I worried you wouldn't be able to walk normally—much less, run. But it was more than that. I knew you were asking for help way beyond what the doctors could give you.

Jim brought me to my emotional knees with that decision. That one event began a deep shift and a new kind of trust between us. After that day, we stood on higher ground—together.

Eventually, I was able to run again. And a whole new universe of experience opened to me.

One technique I have developed is to meditate while I'm running. As I got involved in making the documentary, I would visualize scenes that we needed to shoot to tell the story. As with writers who say they are doing their best work when they let their words flow from the subconscious, my running meditations help me think through problems and find innovative solutions.

But, first, my accident opened conversations with my family at the dinner table.

Lauren said, "I think there was a point in time—I understand you say this was your passion—but I don't think you found a balance between your family and Call. And I think for a while you let it completely take over your life. That's hard. It was hard on me."

Kim added, "I'm kind of with Lauren. I've known for a while that it's become so much better than it was. But some time ago, you were so consumed when Call first came home. You were trying to

We Schapers often express our feelings with honesty around the dinner table (or around a bonfire on the beach).

get him on the proper treatment. I sometimes felt you doted on him and did so much more for him. You focused your attention off your immediate family because you were so fixated on fixing Call. And I think that might have been a growing period for you, too."

My answer was "In a way, I can understand how you all feel. But somebody had to do it. And he never had that chance when he was growing up."

Lauren responded, "I know you said he never had that chance with your parents, but it wasn't your job to do that for him."

"He's my brother" was all I could say. "Think about it. If it was Kim, wouldn't you want the best for her? If you found her? And Kim, wouldn't you do everything you could if it was Lauren?"

"I agree," Lauren said. "I love you, Mom, but I don't think we'll ever win with this situation. I'm not sure you'll ever see it the way we do."

"I had to do what I had to do. He had lost so many years."

"I think there was tension in the family," Kim said. "Because I remember when you'd be gone and you'd be helping Call. Dad, Lauren, and I—we'd be frustrated—and we would talk about it. You weren't here, but we'd say Mom loves Call more than she loves us. She's putting all this energy into Call, and we felt like you weren't even acknowledging us. We had that talk a few times."

I said, "When you feel like a person is hurting, and needs help, and didn't get the help that he needs? Of course. How could you say no to that? Sorry, guys. I feel you all should give me the support for what I had to do for him."

"I think we have," Jim said.

"You have," I admitted. "But why are you saying the things you're saying now?"

"Because it's the way they feel, Rebecca," he said. "And when your father was still alive, he was number one. Everybody else, including the girls and me, came second. We talked about that, and you agreed with that. And we've also talked about this. This was a repeat with Call."

I guess, looking back, there's probably one thing I would change. I would sit my family down and say, "Guys, I'm just going to tell you right now. I'm going full blast with this. I love you guys very, very much. And you're just going to have to accept what I'm going to do. Because I have faith. I know that Call is going to get better. And nothing is going to stop me. And I need your support, all of you. And if I have your support, I know I can go on."

We have these intentions, as though we could write our own life stories before we live them. But as we come to know, God has other plans.

Jim says that after the accident I started to "dabble" in the spiritual realm. I don't know whether I thought of it as spiritual then. I certainly didn't think of it as dabbling. I always had the sense that we are surrounded by supernatural beings and forces. But up to that point, I hadn't felt in touch with them.

After my recuperation, I was running along listening to the birdsongs and smelling the intense fragrance of the blooming jasmine and honeysuckle. As I ran onto a wood footbridge, I noticed a cardinal sitting on the railing. The bird seemed to be looking at me.

I stopped to remember the first time those birds seemed significant to me.

In my searching, I'd been given a psychic reading. The seer advised me to pay attention to cardinals. She said that every time I saw one, my paternal grandmother Corinne was with me. She would be there helping me in some way. After the reading ended, I got into my car to run an errand. I was turning the corner at the end of the street when suddenly a cardinal flew right in front of me.

From then on, I began seeing cardinals a lot. I tried to be receptive to any message the bird might be sending me in the moment. I couldn't put it into words, but the notion that I was being guided and counseled was itself a huge comfort.

Then, one day when I was running near our beach house, I had my first sighting of a hawk. That is, it was my first *meaningful* sighting. I'd seen hawks before, but this time the presence of the bird took on a personal magic for me. It circled and circled above me as I ran. It swooped close and then flew off, far enough that I thought it had gone. Then it came back. The hawk seemed to be teasing me, not just wanting my attention but trying to engage me in a nonverbal conversation.

The message I got, the intuition that flitted into my mind, was that the hawk was a manifestation of Call's spirit. I've said how we'd be thinking of each other and one of us would pick up the phone. Or pay a visit on impulse. Here was another way he'd visit me.

I started seeing hawks all the time. I recorded the sightings in a journal, and I bought books about animals as messengers. I'd spot the hawks at crucial times, most often during periods of conflict, difficulties, sadness, and change—or when an important decision had to be made. It wasn't that there was an explicit message, more the sense that I was being guided and protected, even as I was called upon to nurture and support Jim, my daughters, and Call.

As I began to be more aware of the animals that appeared in my life, I thought of my maternal grandmother Frances. When I was a little girl, it used to amuse her when I'd bring animals into her house. It could be a dog or a kitten or a wounded bird. Once, I proudly brought her a frog! She never fussed about it or scolded me. She was lenient and understanding in ways my mother never was, and I now realize that, of all my family members as I was growing up, quiet and wise Frances was the only one who could teach me unconditional love—the only one except Call, that is.

I never found a snake to take to Frances, but it wasn't because I feared them. I had two snakes as pets!

One day not long after my accident and what I might call my spiritual turning point, three different snakes appeared to me on separate occasions, all in the same day. The first encounter was early in the morning, just outside my kitchen door on the garage-side entry. Later that day as I was running, another snake slithered onto the path directly in front of me. I thought perhaps I should try to lift it or at least nudge the snake with my toe to move it away. More cautious than ever about vehicles by now, I was afraid a biker might run over it. As I moved toward the snake, it veered off and disappeared into the woods. Having seen the two snakes, I thought, *Well, if these are messengers for me, let me see another one.*

As I resumed my run, sure enough, farther along, I saw the same type of snake cross the path in front of me as if on cue! Then, to compound my surprise, I saw two cardinals sitting on a low branch a few feet above me.

I knew I'd had an unusual experience, but I had no idea what it meant. I was sure, because those cardinals had shown up, that I was supposed to pay attention and look for a message in it all.

I hit the books to find out what sightings and visions of snakes might mean in the metaphysical world. To the ancient Greeks, two snakes intertwined on the winged staff of the caduceus was the instrument of Asclepius, the god of healing. You've seen the caduceus countless times—in drugstores and painted on the sides of ambulances. Today, it's the universal symbol of the medical profession.

The snake, therefore, brings healing. It can also symbolize death and rebirth—causing a shift in the way we see the world. Seeing a snake—and appreciating its beauty and power—can offer us a higher and clearer perspective, alerting us to new opportunities to gain wisdom and knowledge.

Then I thought about how a snake grows by shedding its old skin. As this transformation occurs, the snake's eyes are temporarily clouded over before the dead cells are sloughed off.

Years later, the sighting of hawks would become even more significant for me. I have described my first noteworthy sighting of hawks and how they came to mean Call's spirit to me. I return to the meaning of hawks in my life in the epilogue.

Now, how do I relate all this to what was going on in my life? These appearances of animals became a series of revelations for me, which I sensed were turning into something increasingly profound. These events and the insights they inspired affected my outlook, my decisions, and the measures of happiness and joy that came into my life because of my bond with Call and with all of nature.

Earlier that year, before I'd had the accident with the moped, Call was discharged from Pickens Hospital. We had to find a place for him to stay because he'd been evicted from his apartment. I heard about Greer Mental Health Clinic, which is in Greer, South Carolina, about twenty minutes from Greenville. I asked them to arrange an interview for him. Tracy Newton, a clinic counselor, seemed to pick up on Call's gifts. She accepted him into their home facility, which has a residential program for clients. He had to prove he could abide by their rules before they'd recommend he could live independently.

Call's doctors at Greer attributed the severe decline he'd gone through to an imbalance in his medication dosage, coupled with his inability at the time to stay on schedule with taking the drugs. They prescribed a new treatment and put him on a path to long-term stability.

CHAPTER **15**

Return to the Family Home

THEY SAY YOU CAN'T GO HOME AGAIN. YOU MIGHT WORRY that you *shouldn't* go. But I'd say that however painful it turns out to be, you *must* go back to where it all happened.

The healing process starts when you remember—and begin to accept.

Call was then recovering from his decline, under care of the staff at Greer. Even so, he was looking older. His complexion was sallow, and his energy level was low. He'd actually been living in an apartment again. He'd been doing marginally better, but he seemed exhausted.

Around that time, I believe it was in 2008, Call and David and I went back to see the family home on Chanticleer Drive.

As we stood outside the house about to go in, David said, "It's going to be, ah, weird looking at it."

"Yeah" was all I could say as the tears came. My feelings were mixed, to say the least. I was the one who suggested we go back

The Richmond family home on Chanticleer Drive.

there. We were shooting a scene for the documentary. The scene would help us fill in some gaps in the story.

Both of my parents had died in this house, and now someone else owned it. This sprawling, comfortable red-brick residence on a street lined with lush shade trees was now the scene setting for some other family's life story.

It wasn't like we were looking for ghosts. It was a bright, sunny afternoon—not the classic dark and stormy night—and you'd think we were going back for a light-hearted event like a family reunion picnic.

I wanted to go inside—I felt led to go in there. I knew it would bring up old feelings for me—for all of us—and my hope was our visit would be a healing experience. We didn't give the current residents a lot of information—just that it had been years, the siblings were getting back together, and we were nostalgic to peek into the place. They didn't have a problem with it. In fact, they offered to go

The three of us stood outside the house and hesitated before going in.

away for a few hours so we could wander through on our own. It was a trusting and generous gesture from people who hardly knew us.

I assumed our thoughts would turn to Mother. We might sense her spirit there. It would be wonderful if we could connect with the young Mary, the vivacious socialite who was hostess to lavish events in that house, the pretty lady in the figure-flattering swimsuit who romped with us in the surf in those home movies. There had been good times, after all. Perhaps I wanted to recapture some of them.

But as I stood there on the sidewalk and considered going in, my thoughts were all about Dad. I realized that he and David had shared a time together here that Call and I didn't know much about. It was only later that I learned David thought of that period as being mostly happy. As David was finishing high school, Dad remarried, and his new wife and her son moved in with them here on Chanticleer.

I hadn't experienced any of that firsthand. Jim and I were then making our own home in Atlanta. I knew more about the lives of some celebrities who were profiled on TV than I did about Dad and his second wife.

What if this visit stirred other feelings? I hesitated. I didn't want to face those experiences I'd had with my father—experiences I could hardly admit to myself, let alone to anyone else.

Call could see how upset I was, and he thought maybe we should skip the visit after all.

"No, no, I'm good. It's good," I insisted.

David finally asked, "You guys want to go in?"

"I don't know," Call said. "I don't think it's a good idea."

"No, I'm good. I appreciate...," I assured him, stroking Call's arm. "Thank you, I know. I'm good."

Call said, "I'm going to look out after you."

Call was the one to open the front door, and the three of us walked into the entryway. We stopped in our tracks, holding back like children who were entering some cave. The idea that there could be ghosts inside didn't seem so far-fetched.

Jim later explained why I had so much trouble going back there: "It was probably not until you focused your energies on helping Call get better that you ever really dealt with your own issues. I remember we were lying in bed one morning and you just blurted it out, all the things your father had done to you when you were young and the impact it had on you. It just came out. That was the first time I had heard about any of this."

Jim knows this happened right after I watched Phil Donahue's talk show. The participants discussed sexual abuse, and I thought, *Oh, my God, that happened to me!*

Jim described my dad this way: "Call Sr. was a pretty big guy—six-four, a couple-hundred pounds, I guess. Absolute, one hundred-percent control freak. Generally, just a real asshole."

Dad introduced me as his "date" at a party.

Among the old photos, there's a snapshot of Dad in a suit sitting next to me on a couch. I was about fourteen and wearing a crisp white blouse and a miniskirt. I hate that picture—because it was right before an event. My mother should have gone with him to a party, and she didn't. She *couldn't.* My father invited me. I remember his introducing me with "This is my date." I just felt so violated at that party.

Call, David, and I were standing in the living room at Chanticleer.

"After girl-boy parties," I began to tell them as the memories flooded back, "Dad would wake me up and make me dance with him—right here in the middle of the room."

"Oh, God," Call said.

I told them how Dad would take me into the bedroom with my mom being there—maybe asleep, maybe passed out, or not—and he and I would lie down. I'd be in the middle, and he'd be on the other side. I don't know if my mother knew, but she had to have known some of the time. I thought, *Who is this person? He's not my father.*

Other times, he would do things to try to scare me and draw me into their bedroom. Like he'd bang on the window on the outside, hit the screen against the window at midnight. He would know that I would get up and come into the bedroom where my mom and dad were. Sometimes I would just lie there in my own bed and try not to hear it.

The abuse lasted for five years, from when I was eleven to about sixteen. It was during this time that Mother was undergoing shock treatments for paranoid schizophrenia.

That's what came up for me at the house. I regretted the decision to go there, but then I realized the only way to heal is to go *through* the hurt—not around it.

One day as I listened, Jim explained to Kim and Lauren about how he felt after learning about Dad abusing me. He told them, "After I found out what happened between your grandfather and your mother, I was in a really tough spot. Because if I had done what I wanted to do, we would never have seen him again. He would have had no contact with any part of our family. And if I could've cut his balls off, I would've. But by hurting him, that would have, frankly, destroyed your mother."

Lauren asked, "Did you ever confront him or say anything? I mean, I've never heard this. How did you walk into the house and bite your tongue? Did you ever talk to him or say anything to him?"

"No," Jim replied. "I had a choice I had to make. Keep my mouth shut, bite my tongue. Or force your mother to walk away from the one remaining parent that she had."

"Yes, I know," I said. "That was very difficult."

"No, you don't know," Jim countered. "You'll never know. But that's not the point. And I don't expect you to."

Despite the abuse, I felt I still wanted that love from my father—and you do forgive. You so much want a normal, father-daughter relationship. And yet it was not normal.

Jim explained it better than I could: "After his wife died and he was on his own, when push came to shove, if he needed anything, at any time, you would drop everything and take care of him. You just would do that. And I, yeah, I had a very difficult time understanding and wrapping my head around how you could still care so deeply about someone who had done to you what he had done. And, yeah, it was difficult over the years to have to deal with a guy who had sexually abused a child who is now my wife."

In 1988, nearly eighteen years after the abuse, I approached my father about it for the first time. I asked him, "Why, why did you abuse me? Why?" His excuse was because he had always had headaches. He blamed it on the drug he took for it. That was bullshit, and I knew it.

And when I confronted him about it again, he still refused to say anything about it.

Jim saw how my father's refusal to admit his guilt affected me. "Your relationship started to change at that point, when he refused to take responsibility," Jim said. "You stopped coddling him. And you started dealing with him for what he was."

I was not going to let what he had done conquer me. I was not going to let it eat away at me. I made a choice not to do that. I made a choice not to give my power to him.

A few months later, on July 14, 1988, my father wrote a letter, then he walked into the shower, dressed in his Sunday best. He pointed a gun at his heart and pulled the trigger—putting a bullet into his already broken heart.

Jim explained, "What changed for me after his suicide is I didn't have to deal with it anymore. I didn't have to walk into a room with, and I didn't have to go to the beach with, a guy who had sexually abused my wife."

Everybody was asking me, "Why aren't you angry? You should be angry." But I couldn't be angry. I loved my father.

Jim said, "You get emotionally sucked into this relationship. It's very difficult to break away from that. But when he died, that all ended."

In his suicide letter, Dad wrote:

> I do not know where it all started to go wrong. Perhaps it was my grief. I had always thought I was a responsible person but somehow it went wrong. I suffered, I persevered. I think I reached character, but I don't believe I reached hope.
>
> Many people have been so kind, but I am alone in ways that are not explainable.
>
> In my talks with Call, he said I was never a very happy person.

After my mother died, my father had entered another phase of his life. I was involved from time to time. As Jim has said, I'd jump whenever he phoned to say he needed something. He and David were living together on Chanticleer, and, as David has said, it seemed to him they behaved like roommates, each with his own activities and occasionally sharing a meal.

It was during this time that Dad began seeing Millie, the woman he would eventually marry. She and her youngest son Guy were living in Atlanta then, and it didn't take Dad long to invite her to move in with him in Greenville. David remembered:

> I don't recall exactly when he and Millie started contacting each other. She'd been a high-school friend of both our parents. It seems to me that Millie was the first to reach out to Dad. I remember that her husband Jack had died of a heart attack or cancer just before our mom died. This is when Dad's focus turned toward Millie. He was happy then. He acted like a kid in high school with a new girlfriend. We were spending a lot less time together. He would travel to Atlanta to see her frequently, so I would be at the house by myself. It was very common for me to have buddies over for parties when he was gone. Dad seemed good, normal, and happy to me then. I don't recall any moments of depression or odd behaviors until after Millie left him.

It didn't take all that long for Dad to drive Millie away. It was another loss, perhaps the last straw for him. David went on:

> In 1979, I was a senior in high school when Millie and Guy moved in with us. I liked them both from the start. I remember how I enjoyed it when we all went on short vacation trips to Tate Mountain. Millie was always very happy when we were there. She was a pretty cool person.
>
> One time up at Tate Mountain, Guy and I went frog gigging (spear-fishing). This may have been some time before Millie married Dad. I recall that I was having trouble peeling the skin off the frog's legs that day. I was using pliers while wearing gloves, and I was struggling with it. Millie took the legs from me, and, barehanded, she bit down on the skin from the severed legs. She just zipped that skin right off! Whoa! I had

instant respect for her, and I held her in high esteem from then on.

What I wasn't crazy about was all the redecorating she was doing in our family home. I suppose it was because it seemed she was erasing Mom. Plus, I had pleasant memories of just Dad and me living there—as we had done after Mom died—when it was just the two of us as roommates in the house. But Dad liked seeing her happy, and I was moving off to college. I felt that there was no need to make a big deal out of it.

Looking back, we all seemed happy. The only arguments I recall were over Dad's disciplining Guy. Millie was very protective of her son. She seemed to resent any attempt Dad tried to make toward fathering him. And Guy knew how to use it as leverage. He tended to want to drive a wedge between Millie and Dad. Dad knew it, too, and I think he resented Guy for it. I think Guy also resented being uprooted from Atlanta. I can fully understand that. I would not be surprised if his older siblings were supporting him in that feeling as well.

I started Georgia Tech in the summer of 1980. I know it was sometime after I left for Tech that Dad and Millie separated, intending to divorce. I had been barely accepted at Tech. One of the conditions of my acceptance was that I had to start school that summer. I don't have any memories of their deciding to separate. When I look back, I feel that poor Guy got the brunt of all that mess. It must have been truly awful for him.

After Millie left, so did Guy, and Dad rented out the spare bedrooms to a young couple who had a baby. He mostly kept to himself. During this time, my brother Call was still in the Greenville area, before he went away for so long. He was living with friends, sometimes in a cabin in the woods. And he'd show up on Chanticleer occasionally, mostly when he needed money. These brief meetings would often end in a fight—angry words if not blows. Then, a few months later, Call Jr. just disappeared.

David was at school at this point, and I was living in Atlanta with Jim. Our contact with Dad was minimal. He no longer had friends, so I have no doubt he was preoccupied with himself and his despair. How often did he think about what he had done? Did he feel responsible for Mother's depression and suicide? Was he sorry he'd abused her? And us?

Time passed. David graduated from Tech, he married Shari, and they moved to Michigan. Then we got the news Millie had died.

David remembered:

> By that time, Dad had been living alone for some while. I know he was torn up because Millie left him. I remember he was never able to put together in his mind exactly why she left or wanted to divorce him. He was never happy after his separation and divorce from her. After it all happened, he became more introverted.

As I've said, David is a devout Christian, and he felt his faith might offer Dad some comfort.

David told me:

> I had a conversation with Dad about his relationship with God. But he said, "I have done things I cannot be forgiven for. I have been too bad a person to be forgiven." I had no idea at that time what he could have been referring to. I tried to tell him, "God's forgiveness is greater than anything we could ever have done. None of us deserve God's gift of grace. If we did, then we could save ourselves by being good. What Jesus did on the cross would have been for nothing." Still, Dad was convinced there was no redeeming him.

At the time of this conversation, David didn't yet know about Dad's history of abusing me, much less Kim. David may have suspected that Dad's sense of guilt had to do with his wartime experiences. I knew, as perhaps no one else did (unless he'd confided in Millie), how much hurt Dad had caused.

David said:

> When Dad died, I got a call from the couple who lived with him. They found him in the shower after he'd shot himself. I was so full of emotions and anger that I threw a chair across the room. During those six to eight months surrounding Dad's suicide, I had changed careers. Shari and I had moved from Michigan to North Carolina, then we moved again as we bought our first house in Greenville, not all that far from where Dad was. Shortly after the move, we became pregnant with our first child, Andrew. From articles I've since read, in less than one year, we hit five of the top life events that cause toxic stress in a person. I was so stressed that, through the winter and spring following Dad's death, I could not get out of bed. I had trouble doing even the most basic of tasks. I seemed devoid of all energy.
>
> I needed help to get past the depression and grief. I decided to see a Christian counselor, and that helped. But then Andrew was born in May of 1993, and all the depression just seemed to go away. The funk seemed to finally dissipate.
>
> Shari and I wanted to do our best to have a solid, loving family life for our kids. I resolved to take only the good memories of our family growing up, and I would emphasize those. We didn't hide our past from them, but we chose not to discuss the family history. We decided not to share the tough stuff until our children were old enough to understand and accept the facts without distress. We focused on the good times. And a lot of those happy memories revolved around our childhood beach trips and all the laughs we shared.

David latched onto those snapshots and home movies of our family vacations at DeBordieu. I suppose that even today my favorite place to be is at our beach home, just a few miles from there.

When I think about our family's soul contracts, my father's mission is the most difficult to understand and accept. I've come to think that he was born outside of his time. The world he grew up in—and the one he was compelled to fight in—was not a place where he could express himself. He perpetuated the belief that big boys don't cry. He was outwardly loving at times, but he held all his own pain inside.

Most significantly—and this was his pride as well as his anguish—to shield his comrades in battle, he offered his body as a target for German snipers. In doing so, he embraced both courage and terror. And in fighting back, he must have discovered his own rage and brutality.

As with many of the veterans returning from the war, he was expected to make a career and start a family. And he achieved both of those things. Dad made money, and he fathered three children. He took his place in society, and he founded a home. When my mother's illness destroyed her and devastated us, he struggled to maintain a balance that was impossible for him to achieve.

I believe it has been my mission—as it was also Call's—to bring light to Dad's darkness. If not for him, then for others who are tormented. You could say that Dad failed to fulfill his soul contract because he chose to end his life before he could make peace with his torments—before he could find his pathway to healing. As well, you could say that Call and I were prevented from helping him do that. So, that portion of our mission is incomplete.

We are left with one of the most profound and paradoxical questions humans can ask: *Why is there evil in the world?*

One answer—told to our ancestors as if they were little children—is that evil beings are wrestling with God for control of the world.

A more enlightened notion might be that, without evil, there is no way for goodness to evolve. As evil engages with good, it forces transformation. The interplay is the engine of change. Without that dynamic, the engine would stop. Nothing would change.

And if there's anything we can say for sure about the universe, it is that it's always changing, always evolving.

But to embrace that wisdom in a moment of pain? For us humans, that is next to impossible.

When my brothers revisited the house on Chanticleer with me, I could sense something from the expression on David's face. He still didn't believe that Dad, for whom he had mostly fond memories, could have done those things to me.

Later, I confronted David and told him how much his denial of my story upset me.

Then, when he found out about what Dad had done to Kim, there was a shift in our relationship, a milestone in our contracts. David finally believed me, and so began a new chapter in the story of his own healing.

CHAPTER 16

Kim's Path to Recovery

After Kim's treatment at Renfrew in Florida in 2006 and our invigorating trip with Lauren to Europe the following year, Kim seemed stronger. We thought she was on the come-back trail.

As I have done, Kim found solace and renewed self-confidence in running every day. She went from her own program of rigorous exercise to becoming certified as a personal trainer. She set that as a career goal. Kim began to teach fitness classes, and she took on private clients whom she saw in a workout room she'd had built in the basement of her home.

Moderation was not her thing. Kim started two businesses. As she threw herself into her own demanding fitness routine and increased the pace of her professional practice, she became exhausted—physically and emotionally.

All through her young-adult life, Kim's distress had also expressed itself in difficult relationships. As she explains it:

> My eating disorders, mental-health issues, depression, and destructive relationships all served a purpose at the time. They were a means to escape my reality of feeling unsettled and broken within. There were times when I was insecure, uncertain, ambivalent, and vulnerable. The universe often

> attracts to us reflections of how we feel inside. During those times, I attracted men who were unhealthy, controlling, and manipulative.

She eventually thought she'd stabilized and was ready for marriage. She'd dated such domineering men in college, and the pattern continued after she'd made some progress in therapy.

She met a man who charmed her, an effect he apparently had on lots of women. After they married in 2008, Kim continued to work. She resumed her fitness practice, and she was the breadwinner for the two of them. Although he talked of grand schemes and business ventures, he rarely brought home any money. Jim had grown suspicious of him, and so had I.

It was baby sister Lauren who, data drilling in Facebook, found that Kim's husband was still carrying on other intimate relationships.

It was Monday, December 6, 2010. Rather than phone Kim after learning about her errant husband, Lauren (wisely, I think) confided in Jim and me. It didn't take us long to decide that we needed to tell Kim. She and her husband were living nearby in Atlanta then. We decided to invite Kim over. She was scheduled for a therapy session that day, and we told her to skip it. We sat her down and told her about her husband's double life. She fell to the floor in shock. When Kim got up, she was furious. The four of us planned how she would confront him. I won't go into the details, but the situation got pretty heated. We ended up hiring a private investigator to accompany us for protection when the showdown finally occurred.

Only later did I remember that December 6 was the date my mother had committed suicide.

We all encouraged Kim to leave Mr. Wrong, and she did. Fortunately, there were no children involved, and Jim and I helped her take legal and financial precautions so that this guy would not be allowed to reenter or disrupt her life.

Post-breakup, Kim's struggles had just begun. She cried most mornings. She threw herself back into her running—not just around the block but in triathlons. She found a new therapist. She'd kept her house through the divorce. But even though having familiar things around her should have been a comfort, Kim confessed she often didn't want to return home. She couldn't bear to see the condiments he'd left in the refrigerator, but she couldn't bring herself to throw them out. She told us she couldn't bear to touch the things he'd touched, and she insisted we throw them out for her. We repainted the house, and she hired an interior decorator to help her redo the place. Her haven was still the workout room. She remembered happy moments with her clients down there, and she said she regarded it as an emotionally nurturing space separate from the rest of the house.

Then she had a series of not-much-better romantic flings. And despite all the work on the house, she moved—several times. She had false starts and setbacks in the business, and eventually she hit another emotional wall.

In 2013, Kim landed in her last rehab program, three months at Brookhaven, an in-patient facility for women in Tennessee.

It's been years since Kim was treated at Brookhaven, and I can say with confidence that she's found herself. She says she's forgiven her grandfather—something I wrestled with for the longest time—and she's at a healthy weight with a slim figure, looking prettier and more fit than ever.

Having made so many of the mistakes herself, today she's a personal fitness and development coach with a thriving practice.

Courtney Buchanan

Kim, confident and radiant in her recovery.

Kim has found forgiveness, not only for her grandfather but also, more importantly, for herself. And I think, because of Kim, Jim and Lauren and I have all found a new level of forgiveness for each other.

One remarkable thing Kim has shared with us is her frankness. Whereas Call's grip on reality was elusive, Kim has learned to confront the world squarely. She has come to a place where she is truly honest with herself. And she demands honesty from others. She knows when someone is hedging, avoiding the truth. She will want to know what is challenging the person, to understand exactly what is not being said. She stands in her own truth, demanding integrity and accountability of herself and others.

This is a remarkable outcome for a young woman with her personal history and anguish—complicated by a family history of mental illness and abuse.

Kim's story might not seem all that relevant. It's a sidelight on Call's struggles mainly because her problems show how a kind of curse can move through a family from one generation to the next.

But I'm also thinking of blessings. I don't believe Kim could be the person she is today—with her strength of character and her wisdom about personal development—without the trials she's undergone.

Through Kim, I've come to see how our family functions best as a unit—and how it seems fated and by design that we should share this life journey, nurturing each other's experiences and development.

In our family, I am able to stand back, seeing things from many perspectives, as if through the lens of a camera. Our other daughter Lauren is the one who dives into a situation to dig for every detail, until she reaches the bottom, to gather all the facts. Kim is the one who demands not only that all must be revealed and known but also that the life lesson must be found, learned, and applied. It is always Jim who listens to us all, carefully hearing everything we've discovered, so he can then apply his brilliant logic to the situation.

Finally, I take it all away to consider and reflect upon. I'm the one who weaves it all more gently together by going within, by applying heart.

This intimate interaction is, I've come to think, the essence of a soul group. With overlapping and complementary gifts, we've developed the ability to use them in ways that serve, support, and empower us all.

Coming together over Kim's struggle empowered us as a single *energy being*. We nurtured her as I had nurtured Call. Although they'd been wary of him and not entirely supportive of my commitment to him, with Kim we found a focus at our center, an immediate and irrefutable challenge. In overcoming it, the love we shared expanded.

If Call had come back into our lives later, perhaps he'd have been welcomed warmly. But had he not been with us earlier to impart important life lessons, perhaps we wouldn't have made it this far.

Chapter 17

The Schapers Come Together and Reflect

"There's nothing worse than seeing your mother break down, emotionally just exhausted and vulnerable," Kim said. "At the time, I didn't understand what was going on. I know that I loved my grandfather. I knew that I loved going over there. I loved going over there for Christmas. He'd give me these big teddy bears. And he was a loving man. There are a lot of things I did when I was little and never understood why. It was perplexing and it was embarrassing. I never thought about saying anything until I got into therapy, into treatment. I felt like it wasn't normal. I don't know."

While she was in therapy for her anorexia, Kim revealed that she'd been sexually abused by her grandfather. She said it had gone on for years, from ages five to nine.

Jim hadn't known. None of us had. He learned about it this way: "I was in Philadelphia. I was at the airport. I was getting ready to get on a flight. I called you to find out how Kim was. She'd had a therapy session that day. And you told me. I sat down in a chair, missed my flight, missed the next flight. That was the worst day of my life."

One night at dinner after Kim's recovery, Lauren asked me, "Can I ask you something? Not to put you on the spot, but how did you not know he would do that to her? Or to me?"

I just never thought my father would do something like that.

That evening, Lauren asked the same question of Jim. His reply was "I have no excuse. That's what I live with every day. I have no excuse. I should have known better. And I didn't."

Kim insisted, "But I don't hold that against anybody."

"I know you don't," Jim responded. "But I do. And that's mine. And I do. You should never have been left in that house alone. Knowing what your mother knew and what I knew. Never in a million years. And that's my problem."

"It's fine" was all Kim could say.

He disagreed, "It's not fine. And it never will be fine. That's what you'll never understand. The guy was a pedophile."

"But I'm fine now," Kim told him.

"It doesn't matter, Kim," Jim said. "Because both you and Lauren, what you don't understand is that what he did to Kim affected all of us. It wasn't just you. You obviously the most. But the byproduct of what he did affected the entire family for an extended period of time. You may be fine now—and you are—but the journey you took, no girl should have to take that journey. None. It should never, ever happen. And, yeah, as they say, what doesn't kill you makes you stronger. But that doesn't make it right. It doesn't make it right."

How did we miss that?

Later, Kim remembered, "I think, for me, people think, *Doesn't she have hate toward him? How can you not have so much hate toward someone who violated you that way?* I felt hate at one time, and I think that's a total emotion to go through. Now it's more of

Lauren asked, "How did you not know he would do that to her? Or to me?"

forgiveness and more of pity toward him. And I will say, for a while there, I had so much fear that I was going to do the same to my kids. I don't know why. I know I would never. But now that I'm so far into the process, I know that I would never even think about it. That fear is gone."

I told Kim I had forgiven him. I wasn't sure I could forgive myself for what happened to her. But I watched Kim heal as she let go of her resentment.

When Kim was in therapy, it struck me how threads of unhappiness and pain have run through our family—abuse, voices, alcoholism and addiction, eating disorders, depression, schizophrenia, and suicide. It seemed obvious that the mental illness, at least, went back generations. The other conditions and disorders had surrounded and engulfed us to the point where it became difficult

Asked about our failure to foresee the abuse, Kim insisted, "But I don't hold that against anybody."

to separate cause from effect. Each disorder amplified the pain of the other family members and their woes in what became a chorus of anguish.

What's more, the boundaries between our suffering as individuals were blurred. For example, I didn't suffer from schizophrenia—I didn't hear voices or have hallucinations—but I shared Call's anguish. My suffering was not as intense, but there was no denying I shared his pain.

How do you heal sickness when it encompasses the whole family? For sure, it's not just a matter of one person taking a few pills.

Here was an insight that grew deeper the more I thought about it: When one family member is afflicted, the whole family has a problem. You might say, of course, it's a problem that affects and wounds and tortures all of them.

But that's not what I mean, not at the deeper level. What I mean is, *the person's affliction arose* ***because*** *the family has problems.*

Take, for example, the abuse Kim suffered. That kind of violation was shared by me and by Call, at the hands of our father. Again, we weren't sure Call had been abused physically, but his emotional scars were deep. I suppose Dad was acting out his pain from loss of the love and affection of his wife, post-traumatic stress from wartime, and sexual abuse by an adult when he was a boy. And those are just the causes we know—or can at least guess.

Yes, there's a group psychology at work here, a situation that might invite the attentions of social workers and psychiatrists. Those avenues of help didn't seem to hold much promise as I wondered how to both help Kim and heal our family. Yes, we'd deal with her eating disorders on a symptomatic level. We'd get her eating right and get her settled into a discipline so she could take care of herself. Her caregivers would teach her to maintain—as I had struggled just to get Call's condition stabilized so he could maintain a routine existence.

My intuition told me that the approaches of psychology and sociology could help Kim take steps on the ladder but would never get her to the top. One day, Kim might seem cured, but she'd only be maintaining. If her suffering was a symptom of generational struggle within our family, making that climb on her own wouldn't help the rest of us heal. We all needed to be lifted up—*together.*

With that realization, I turned to books on spirituality. I consulted metaphysical practitioners and professionals who had reputations as healers. I talked to psychics, astrologers, medical intuitives, life coaches, and modern-day shamans. It was remarkable how similar their mindsets were. They were no strangers to the notion of soul contracts, which assumes reincarnation, perpetual return, karmic issues, and life missions.

A new insight they gave me put a name to my curiosity about threads within families. They called it *tribal consciousness.* I learned that it could apply not just to my immediate family but also to groups, communities, political movements, races, nations—and even to the whole planet.

But, you may ask, how is this information useful? How would it apply to helping Kim get back on her feet? How could it help her rejoin our family circle and help us all heal?

One definition is that tribal consciousness is a set of beliefs shared by a group of people. A characteristic of tribal thinking is that members of the tribe are unquestioningly loyal to those beliefs. When my father went to war, he went on behalf of his tribe—our country. His faith in its beliefs—his patriotism—was never in question. Dad proved this by his actions.

Now, people can argue whether those beliefs were—and are—appropriate or not. Maybe truth doesn't even enter into it. The key test is whether those ideas work for the tribe. The proof is whether adhering to those beliefs ensures the tribe's survival.

They say tribal beliefs are mostly lies, but they are useful lies. Greek mythology served its purpose for thousands of years. The psychiatrists even have a technical term for mythical beliefs that are nevertheless useful—*heuristic fictions.* For example, if I believe I'm a good person, I'm more likely to take actions that I and other people consider to be good. The question of whether I'm truly good is pointless. And, on a practical level, my life is a series of actions, some you'd consider good and some not. But, as I say, it's useful for me to believe that I'm good—and that my tribe will benefit from my actions.

Oh, I know all this is starting to sound esoteric, but I'll bring it home—to my home—and back to Kim.

When I was growing up, the useful fiction in my father's house was that the Richmonds were an affluent, socially connected, healthy, handsome, and happy family. To the outside world, no matter how deep my mother sank into depression and substance abuse, no matter what kinky pleasures my father sought from me, no matter whether our mother and his son were both paying attention to voices that spoke only inside their heads, no matter what horrors we shared privately, it was the mission of our family to maintain appearances and to survive.

You might say that my family's situation was unusually complicated, even for families who have suffered untimely grief.

Consider how any family—your family, perhaps—might react when your teenage son suddenly takes an overdose of pills, but survives. There might be no evident family history of mental illness, no heritage of grief, no immediate, apparent cause other than his recent moodiness and the stresses of growing up.

In any family faced with a new situation like this, the first reaction is likely to be *denial*—typically, a series of denials. First, his parents will deny that the boy has a problem at all. Then they might admit that he has a problem, and he needs to get help. But that help will be limited to addressing the symptoms of a problem they think is uniquely his. Then they will begin to realize the impacts on the family—starting with health insurance, through group counseling, and then possibly into marital misunderstandings and stresses. Yes, the family has a problem, or a series of problems, arising from the necessities of dealing with what could become their son's chronic illness.

What they don't yet appreciate—what it may take them years or maybe never to accept—is that their son's overdose might be self-medication, not just for problems he owned as an individual, but also for a whole swarm of inherited griefs that may go back—probably do go back—for generations in his tribe.

Pundits call some of these stresses *social ills.*

Remember—the tribe perpetuates its existence through shared beliefs. And those beliefs are mostly lies. Put another way, denial is a means of ensuring the tribe's survival.

So, let's go back to where I was standing on the sidewalk with Call and David in front of the house on Chanticleer. I didn't want to go in, even though it was my idea. I had the feeling that walking through those rooms—walking through the memories and the pain that would come up—was the pathway to healing.

As I held Kim's hand though her trials, I was beginning to understand that underlying our family life was a network of intertwined soul contracts. With this awareness came the hope that we are more powerful as a family than we ever could be as individuals—even though, as individuals, we might hope we could work through our problems on our own.

Speaking of and thinking about mental illness as *illness* closes off aspects of the condition that deserve to be explored. Likewise, *dysfunction, disease,* and *ailment* don't get us anywhere in that direction.

When I think of Call, most of all, I think of his *gifts.* He was a *gifted* person. And he used those gifts, whether consciously or not, to help me heal. His influence was also strong on my daughters.

For example, one day, Kim and I were going through some gifts (the kind with wrappings and bows). We were preparing for a surprise party we were giving for Lauren. Kim asked me whether I had any family photos I could give her. For this party, she wanted early childhood pictures of Lauren. So I dug into my trove, and I came across a bunch in a storage box next to the wrapping paper. I handed all of them to Kim, and she said she'd sort through them later.

Kim brought back a picture—not of Lauren but of her. At a glance, it gave me chills. Kim was about five, and she was sitting with Call. Her face beamed a gleeful smile as she sat beside him, his arms encircling her. In her arms, Kim cradled Raggedy Ann and Andy dolls that Call had just given her.

This was one of those times during his long absence when Call had dropped in unannounced—and then just as quickly disappeared. The picture was taken at the house on Chanticleer—when Dad was still alive and we'd joined him to celebrate the holiday.

Gifts—that Christmas, Call had just shown up with those dolls. He must have had very little money back then. Yet he had spent his pocket money on these dolls for Kim.

His special gift was the love he brought her. He opened his heart, and Kim knew she was cherished. She basked in his light.

No doubt this was why, out of that stack of old snaps, she chose this decades-old picture to show me.

I don't remember what Kim might have been going through just then. I'd bet that Call sensed something, that he knew it was time to intervene. As I've said, he always knew when to pick up the phone. His questions were never specific (other than asking me about my patience), but his presence at the other end of the line was palpable. His attention was reassuring.

As to gifts, Call's perceptiveness was extraordinary. Some practitioners I consulted guess that people with schizophrenia often see too much, take in too much, and thus can't cope. They fall into states of sensory overload.

Some of my advisers have gone so far as to say that when an afflicted person is acting out, he might be responding to some paranormal stimulus. When Call was smearing feces on the walls of his apartment, was he responding to waves of grief he was receiving from someone else?

I don't know. Who does? I'm not sure I'd go that far, but I am certain of Call's giftedness. Although he exhibited dysfunctional and self-destructive behaviors at times, he was mostly all about compassion.

As you'd expect, my thoughts were always with Call at Christmastime, even when he wasn't with us. And that's still true now that he's not here in physical, human form.

After Call had passed on to the next plane of existence—and I have only vague notions of where or what that place is—I believe his presence in spirit played a part in our family's transformation.

In December of 2014, two years after Call died, Jim and I and our daughters took a family vacation to Nevis, a small island in the Caribbean. Before that experience, both as a family and as individuals, we'd all followed healing pathways. As souls and as human beings, we'd worked through and gotten to the other side of some significant milestones.

On this trip, I feel we went to the next level as a family unit. We began to discover how effective we could be together—in ways we had not yet imagined.

Kim remembered, "It was an incredible trip for all of us. I, for one, felt closer to my sister than ever. If I go back to reflect on this trip, I smile with joy because I felt it was effortless to be with her. Believe me, the transition we went through to get here was not an easy one."

She continued, "Don't get me wrong, we still bickered at times on this trip, but not as much as on prior vacations. Why, you ask, are we just *now* getting along? Because I believe time has healed a lot of pain."

What happened on that trip? You know, as I try to describe it now, I'm not all that sure. It's not like I can identify a moment or a comment or a gesture that sparked the change. The girls went snorkeling for turtles, and I know they got a kick out of sharing that experience. One evening, we had dinner out on the pier, underneath a spectacularly starry sky. As we sat swathed in the sea breezes, we sipped champagne and opened up to each other.

Lauren's version was "We all sat around sharing intimately what bothered us the most about one another. We also told each other what we saw as their best quality or attribute. I think in past trips, we wouldn't have been able to do that without someone getting their feelings hurt."

I can't point to any one thing anybody said. I do remember that Kim confessed to Lauren how much she resented and felt hurt by a comment Lauren had made in front of other people. Apparently, Kim had harbored this resentment for some time.

Kim confessed to Lauren:

> There was this situation. I was sitting in front of you in a meeting. You said to a woman sitting next to you, "Yeah, that's my sister in front of us. I never want to be like her." That struck me. It struck hard. And, Dad, you defended her comment, and I will never understand why it seemed you took her side. Comments like those made me feel judged.

And turning back to Lauren, Kim added:

I felt as though I had to walk on eggshells around you. I knew you harbored a great deal of resentment toward me from childhood. You felt left out, even unheard. And I believe you feel like a lot of that was due to my illness. I recognize that I took a lot of time and attention from you so I could get help.

Lauren responded:

It seems almost every year on these trips there has been something disruptive going on for one of us. One year it would be you struggling with your eating disorder. Another time it would be one or both of us dealing with the heartbreak of a recent breakup. And I confess I can come across as controlling, downright bossy to you. What changes the dynamic is when we can laugh. I realize, even as we're on some trip where we're both arguing and laughing, I have accumulated a lot of good memories that can never be replaced.

And this year's trip to Nevis has been different from all the others. I don't know if it's just a result of our maturing, growing within ourselves. Or, more importantly, perhaps we're more content with where we are in our lives. From my standpoint, I think this is the happiest, the most content I have ever seen you, Kim. This shift in you made it much nicer to be around you. It was easy to interact with you more gently and lovingly. I would also say that this is probably the least controlling I have been. I know that alone had to make it nicer for you to be around me, as well. It doesn't seem like older-younger sister now. We're on a more equal footing with each other.

Kim told her:

It seems you've finally been able to let it all go. I'm not exactly sure why. Maybe you're more mature? You're more tolerant of human growth because you're experiencing your own newfound life? Whatever the reason, I don't feel the judgment

> as much as I once did. I feel like you want to hang out with me. You want to know the whole Kim. You don't avoid me or carry around opinions about where I've been. I think you now understand that when someone goes through a difficult situation, it may be almost impossible for you to understand why they handled it the way they did. By now, you've experienced some of your own obstacles and heartbreaks. Now you appreciate there isn't one right way to do things. Life is navigating, exploring, developing, and growing—with some hiccups along the way. It isn't a straight line. It's not like everybody can go to college, secure a successful job, get married, and have kids. I'm coming up on my second marriage—and still no kids. I have a fabulous career that I never studied or trained for. This is who I am now. I really appreciate that you can, at last, enjoy me for who I am today. I love you. I know I will often wonder when will I get to see you next. Before this Christmas vacation in Nevis, I never felt that way. I love you more, and I want us to be closer.

Wow! I had been looking forward to the day when Kim would have worked through her issues and Lauren would be more accepting of her. Here it was.

Here is how Jim reflected on it later:

> The night on the pier in Nevis was nothing short of special. The atmosphere was perfect. We shared our wishes and dreams for the future—with an honesty we'd never had as a family before. The Schaper clan has always been close, given the adversities we've had to face together. But that evening was unique even for a group that had shared so much. Each of us shared our dreams and hopes for the future in a raw but sensitive way that made sharing easy.
>
> Our Christmas vacations over the years have provided some great memories. But there has always been some type of drama

> running through them. Some years, we've taken boyfriends with us—whether they were actually with us or it was just their issues we took as baggage. Some years we focused on Kim's illness. And, of course, that was stressful.
>
> On past vacations, I was never able to fully unwind. Sometimes, I've had to take work with me… But, this year, Kim had not only stabilized, but she was also flowering. Lauren had gotten past a recent breakup and, as Kim told her, seemed more forgiving, more tolerant, of her sister's challenges. And Rebecca seemed to be breathing sighs of relief. She wasn't always running off by herself as she fretted about how she would handle the most recent crisis.

I wrote in my journal that this trip to Nevis was a most auspicious beginning for the next leg of our earthly journey together. We had created greater possibilities for our travels as a family soul group. We'd expanded the appreciation we have for each other. And we were ready to assist, support, nurture, exalt—anything we chose to take on—individually and together.

It was just the four of us. Healed, communicating, loving, and embracing each other—and ready for whatever comes next.

Jim is our rock. In her transformation, Kim has become a therapist and teacher. Lauren is our family navigator. Me, I'm our bridge between the darkness and the light.

Chapter 18

Call's Reawakening

Although Call's recoveries and reversals took place over a span of years, having to deal with the variations in his condition left me emotionally whipsawed.

Now I think back to when Call had that devastating relapse. The most difficult part for me was to manage the disconnect between my hopes and expectations for him and the profound discouragement and exhaustion I felt whenever he lost ground.

It was in the autumn of 2007, and he was in Marshall Pickens Hospital. This was not long after he'd lost his apartment. I visited him as soon as they would let me. He seemed to have taken some responsibility for his actions. He was on meds again, and he seemed lucid.

David and I were in his room waiting for Call to come back after he'd left to have a cigarette.

When Call came through the door, I asked him, "So, how was your smoke break?"

"Pretty good," he said and smiled.

"Do you want to talk a little bit about your stay here and what you worked out?"

Call in an expansive mood (without his dentures).

"Four weeks ago from this past Friday, I had some rough going. Hearing voices. Thoughts running through my head. And the doctor here got the medications straightened out."

I said, "I think we got our brother back, right Dave?"

"Yeah," David agreed.

"I sure hope so," Call said.

"We do," I told him.

"I'm heading home," he said.

"Yeah," I said, "you're on a mission, aren't you? So, tell us about your mission."

"Well, I've been in process. Last Thursday night, I signed my last contract."

"And what did the contract say?"

"You wouldn't understand the words in it," Call insisted. "It's a different language. Not a different language. It's English language, but you wouldn't think it was English by the way it was said. And the Lord the Father handed me my contract, and I signed it. Last Thursday. Let's see, last Thursday, yeah."

Again with the *process!* It was a recurring theme with him. And whether he was talking to God, his own heart of hearts, or just his face in the mirror, the importance for his treatment was that he had made a plan and was vowing to stick to it.

I asked him, "So, your mission here is to stay here for six months?"

"Yeah, right."

"And then, what happens after six months?"

He was referring to his caregiver when he answered, "She says if I've been good, if my behavior's been good, if everything adds up, I can get an apartment."

"I think that's great, Call. I think you're on your way."

"I think it is, too."

He beat his deadline. Call had a new apartment in five months, and I handed him the keys.

"Becky, it looks great. Thank you so much for helping me out."

"Oh, you're so welcome," I said, and I watched him slip the new door key onto his keyring.

"So, that's official for you, Call, right there."

"Sure is."

I wanted Call to have this life. I had this vision. And I realized, once I let go, Call could heal and have his life. But I had to let go. I wanted to move into the background while I continued to support him. I would make sure he had the right meds. I would make sure

I wanted Call to have this life. I had this vision.

he had the right caseworker. I'd do whatever I could just to provide him with everything Call told me he needed.

I told myself it had to be his own journey. If he wanted it, if he needed it, Call had to be responsible enough to ask me for it. By that time, I didn't worry about his being too proud to ask. We were way past that. I wasn't going to fret constantly with mindreading games about what I thought he needed.

Kim said, "I think that was a hard time for you, but it opened up your eyes, knowing that here's this man, older than you are, in his late fifties. He's not a child anymore. He has to learn to take care of himself. That was probably the journey he needed to go through. He needed to hit that rock bottom again. He might not be a hundred percent better, but you were a hundred percent better in your mind knowing that you can't always be there. I feel like that's made a big difference with Call and our connection with you as a family."

One day when Call seemed to have a clear head, I asked him, "What would you tell people who have your illness, Call?"

"To go see a psychiatrist and get started on medication. And *pray*." And he cackled at that, and I joined him.

In that laugh, we shared everything else about it that we'd been through together. Yes, a drug regimen is part of the solution. But even with the right mix and balanced dosage, surviving and coping and beginning to feel good about life involve so much more. It's a matter of motivation, of will. Of resilience and survival toughness. I won't say survival skills because those come in time. No, it's just pure toughness. Call had that. I always knew he did.

Then I asked him, "Do you feel anger that you have this illness?"

I was surprised when he answered without hesitation, "No I don't. Not at all. Not one bit."

"Do you feel fulfilled as a person?"

"Yeah, I do. I surely do. I'm thankful for the people who are around me. Who love and care for me. Really thankful for that."

Two years later, on September 5, 2009, Call was still doing pretty well, and for the first time for him, he attended his high-school class reunion. It was the fortieth reunion of a graduating class of Greenville High. The class of 1969.

I helped Call get his clothes ready, and I ran a batch of things over to the dry cleaners and tailor. "They hemmed everything up for you," I told him. "Light starch on the shirts, which you asked for."

Call was happy about going to the reunion and seeing some of his old friends. I was so proud of him. This was a huge journey for Call. Huge!

Call greets old friends at the Greenville High reunion. He shakes hands with Rev. Stan Johnson as Fletcher Mann Jr. (L) and Rick Farnsworth (R) enjoy Stan's teasing Call about past girlfriends.

He met up with a bunch of them at Como's Pete's No. 4 diner, their old hangout. They swapped stories and joked for a couple of hours.

His buddy Stan quipped, "Maybe there's a couple of girls here who need us to buy drinks."

"Make mine a hamburger with a dill pickle," Call said grinning, ignoring Stan's comment.

But Stan was stuck on the girl angle. "Call, what's going to happen when you run into your high-school girlfriend?"

Call laughed and shook his head. "I don't know what's gonna happen." That was an understatement.

And for someone like him who's in treatment, even if you do the right things and you take your medications, if it's a stressful situation, the voices can still come on. But they didn't.

The big meetup would be the next day. Stan advised Call, "Tell your sister to make sure you get a manicure."

Call shot back, "They're gonna paint my fingernails pink."

I tried to keep calm about the reunion. As I always did when he was setting out on any new experience by himself, I worried whether he would be okay. I checked off the list in my mind. *I've got to make sure about boom-boom-boom-boom.* I just let him be, and that said a lot for me, too.

The next morning as I said good-bye to him and his buddies, Call was duded up in a bright-green golf shirt and khaki pants, with his beard close-cropped and his hair trimmed and combed. His nails were freshly manicured, though not painted pink. He rode with his friends Rick and Stan. I'd rented them a shiny-black Chrysler limousine. I wanted Call to feel he was King for a Day.

Rick said, "Well, this is it, right here! I'm surprised to see so many cars."

"I know it," Call agreed as he swallowed hard. He looked scared.

As the three friends entered the school doors, they passed underneath a banner that read, "Welcome!! Class of 1969. Goooo Greenville!!!"

Rick asked him, "Are you ready, Call?"

"Yeah," he barked back. But he didn't look so sure.

Honestly, I don't know all that what went on in there. I was invited, and I stayed long enough to snap a few pictures of him with his friends. But I decided to let Call be and enjoy this special time. Despite my intense curiosity, I didn't want to play mother hen to a bunch of middle-aged men who were trying to be teenagers for a day. And I didn't want Call to feel he was being watched—at least, not by me.

As to whether any of the "girls" showed up, I don't know that, either. I'd guess it would have taken some courage for any woman to endure all the horseplay and adolescent humor. But I suppose, by the time you have made it forty years past high school, maybe your skin has grown thicker.

I didn't even get a report. Later, I finally decided to ask him how it went. He turned bright red, grinned the biggest smile I ever saw on his face, and he let a long cackle rip.

I guess he made out okay.

Two years after that, in 2011, Call was hospitalized with a broken hip. It became infected and nearly caused his death. He spent six months in the hospital but recovered. Call decided to quit smoking, and he did. He lost some weight, color came back to his cheeks, and I think his health was better than it had ever been since before he went missing.

Leaning on his walker, Call made it up the sidewalk and into our house in Atlanta during May of 2012. Jim presented him with his birthday gift. True to his undying fan loyalty, Jim gave Call a University of South Carolina team sweatshirt.

Choking back my tears of joy, I proposed a toast:

> Dear Call, I never dreamed you would be here on your sixtieth birthday.
>
> Your journey has been incredible.
>
> And you have arrived, here and now, with a magnetism I can't explain. Being with you these last thirteen years has taught me patience and to live in the moment. I don't know what tomorrow will bring. But just you being here with us today is what matters most.

So, I say, Call, let the journey continue to unfold!

Thank you for being you. I love you.

Four months later, on September 4, 2012, Call Richmond Jr. passed from this life.

Call had lived just long enough to see our documentary *A Sister's Call* completed. In his last year, he was strong enough to go with me to some of the screenings. And he got up on stage and answered questions from the audience. The audience loved him, and some of them told me later they thought his words were profound.

Call reminds me from time to time that he's still with me, still looking out for me, still doing his part to make sure we fulfill all the promises we've made to each other.

CHAPTER 19

Lauren Chases the Sun

I'VE SAID LAUREN IS THE NAVIGATOR OF OUR FAMILY, AND, SURE enough, she charted a different course after Call's passing.

You might think that, as the youngest member of the Schapers at the time, Lauren was relatively unscathed by all the hurt that swirled around us. It's true, she was never subjected to the physical abuse and body-image suffering Kim endured. In that way, her plight was similar to David's a generation before. She was at the center of the cyclone but apparently uninjured.

The injuries dealt to Lauren were more indirect and took place mainly within our household. First, as she expressed to me later and Kim agreed, there were the feelings of abandonment and jealousy whenever I'd dash off to care for Call. Second, as we eventually resolved on our trip to Nevis, Lauren was buffeted by the storms in Kim's life, along with the stresses of supporting her recovery. There had always been spats caused by sibling rivalry in their relationship, but these resentments were amplified by the magnitude of Kim's challenges.

So, when as young women they made peace with each other, it was a joyous breakthrough. And they've been incredibly close ever since.

A quality Lauren shares with her sister Kim is forthright honesty. She always says exactly what she thinks. And when Kim was facing difficult decisions, Lauren's opinions often came across as controlling. Her big sister mostly resented Lauren's advice, even if Kim suspected it was sound.

Through it all, despite her opinions and criticisms, Lauren was deeply loyal to the family. And because she was so invested in our welfare, Lauren suffered along with us. Meanwhile, she didn't express the hurt or act out as much as Kim had done. I think this reticence was partly due to pride and partly because Lauren didn't want to compound our grief with her complaints.

Lauren carries her honesty—and, yes, her pride—with grace and beauty. I believe, at her core, she is a serene soul. After all, if we're going to trust a navigator's instructions, we want her to be sure of herself!

In these ways, Lauren had a special affinity with Call.

For one thing, those two shared a love of music. In Call's last hours, our family kept vigil at his bedside. Lauren created a mixtape of his favorites. And as he hovered on the edge of this life, she gently placed the earbuds in his hairy ears. It was an intensely intimate moment in what we all experienced as a sacred event.

Then, after Call was gone, Lauren reported that he showed up in her life repeatedly. She'd be washing dishes and she'd sense he was standing there beside her. She thought back to the times when she accompanied me to Greenville on caregiving visits. One of her regular chores was to delve into the pile of dirty dishes in his sink.

She felt he was there when times were tough, to help her along.

Lauren recalls that his cheerfulness in her conversations with him was itself a source of comfort for her: "'Hey, Lauren!' he'd say, with that big, happy laugh of his. He was always so positive, making me wonder why I was so bent out of shape over something so little. He made me think that these stresses I was feeling weren't all that bad, in the scheme of things. He just put me in a good mood."

Another aspect of Lauren's loyalty to the family is that for a long while she was something of a homebody. Even as Lauren entered young womanhood, she stayed close to Jim and me, preferring her bedroom in Atlanta. Over the years, there had been a few times when she moved out seeking adventures. These mostly had to do with romantic relationships she thought would turn serious, as some did. But these forays ended in painful breakups, after which she'd come back home to us.

Lauren's returning to live with us was never an interruption or a burden. We were thrilled to have her, and I think she was reassured that we'd always provide a safe, loving haven for her.

Two years after Call died, Lauren moved back in with us. She was undergoing a devastating breakup with a man she had been sure was her soul mate. They'd been well on their way to making marriage plans, and then their ship hit the rocks.

A year later, Lauren was holding down a good job in Atlanta. We weren't sure she was ready to embark on a new adventure, but we felt confident she was healing.

So it came as a complete surprise when she announced she'd be moving to California.

Why California? was our first question.

Lauren insisted she'd wanted to move there since she was three. (How such dreams would occur to a toddler might be a question for a psychic. Was this more family karma? We had no idea.)

Not only was Lauren determined she had to live in California, but she was also specific about the city—Santa Monica, on

Gabe Simpson

Lauren on the "Left Coast," thriving in Santa Monica among the palm trees and beaches of Southern California.

the ocean, at the western edge of the sprawling metropolis of Los Angeles County and its thirteen million other residents.

Crazies, more like! (At least, that's how some people "Back East" think of the "Left Coast." What's worse, when you say "USC," they think you mean the University of Southern California, not the University of South Carolina! In my part of the world, we USC Fighting Gamecocks have no particular affection for Trojans.)

As we were soon to find out, Lauren had made a soul connection with a new BFF—Lauren Wood—who had already made plans to move to Santa Monica. That town has become something of a magnet for millennials now that it is a hub not only for the entertainment community but also as the Silicon Beach of high-tech industry.

So it would be Westward Ho! for the two Laurens as they were drawn to the sparkling blue Pacific, expansive beaches, high-priced condos, and hot-guy startup entrepreneurs and the fast-moving investment bankers who bet on those classy crapshoots.

A mother worries!

That's when I asked Call's spirit to stick with Lauren as she embarked on this new adventure.

Sure enough, there were those times in her new place (four blocks from the beach) when Lauren sensed Call standing patiently by her. And tears would come when she'd be driving in her car and—more times than seemed coincidental—his favorite song from the mixtape (the one we'd picked for his funeral service) played on the radio.

When Lauren informed us that she was moving out, it was June of 2015. I had been thinking that I had not seen a hummingbird for months, and this was the time of year when they'd usually be buzzing around the feeders in our backyard.

For a low-key send-off party, we'd invited several of Lauren's friends over for dinner. That evening before we all gathered around the table, she was sitting at the bottom of the back-porch steps with her guests. When Lauren climbed up to the deck, she saw a hummingbird lying there on the stone floor. She called me to come out. We both panicked, assuming that the dear little bird had flown into the sliding-glass door. As I stood there praying it was okay and not knowing what else to do, Lauren took pictures with her phone. Within several minutes, the hummer regained its strength, flew straight to the feeder, and started to eat.

Lauren and I looked at each other and laughed. We both knew immediately it was a message from Call.

When Call was living alone in his little apartment, he had two hummingbird pictures on his wall. He had a special love of hummingbirds. He and I often talked about them during our walks in the woods.

I confided in Lauren that I was so concerned about her move that I'd asked Call's spirit to support her. We took the sighting of this hummingbird as a clear confirmation of my request. And the symbolism seemed to be:

Even when you fall and you lose hope, I will lift you up.

Epilogue

I'M TRYING TO PUT IT ALL TOGETHER. I KNOW THAT THE intertwining of life and spirit is a richer pattern than I can see even now. It's difficult—perhaps impossible—to judge the process while we're immersed in it, while we're still being buffeted by life's flow.

Process! It was Call's favorite word. The way he used it, his process was an agreement and a plan and a journey. It was supposed to be practical and routine, at the level of his treatment plans. But I believe it was also spiritual. I've speculated that Call understood his soul contract better than most of us do. Even if he didn't always express himself in words, he cheerfully accepted his life's mission and its obligations.

Call came back into our lives as a quiet, healing influence for our family, especially for me. I became an integral part of his life, too. I helped him find a way back to his humanity, not simply to what the mundane world would call his *sanity.*

Although it's been years since he gave up his physical body, I still feel Call's presence. In 2015, when Lauren moved to California, I asked Call's spirit for help. I told him he needed to step up to the plate. I needed him to guide her, to be with her, and to send help when she needed it. I prayed that he heard me, and I am sure he answered. Lauren says she has felt him many times. She knows beyond all doubt that Call is there to guide her, and that he will continue to be around her when she needs him. Kim feels the same way.

Call loved nature as much as I do. When we went for walks in the woods, he would name the kinds of trees for me. Now, he communicates to me through animals. I sense Call is with me every time I see a hawk or a hummingbird. I believe that through these creatures, he sends me messages. And I've told you about the special meanings I've found when I encounter snakes.

What are these messages? The animals don't communicate to me in voices, and I can barely put their wisdom into words. Both the kind of animal and the timing of its appearance are revealing. The hawk urges patience, just as Call challenged my impatience often when he saw me. Patience allows events to unfold as they must, allows a period of quiet when the subconscious (which is more directly influenced by the soul) can speak. Patience gives us the space to see things in a larger perspective. (That's why I named our film production company GreyHawk.) A hummingbird is joyous, inventive, curious, and playful. Seeing a hummingbird, Call's favorite bird, pulls me out of my adult judgment, silences my censoring mind, and encourages me to see the wondrous world through the eyes of a child. Hummingbirds help me see beauty and opportunity.

The snake signals impending transformation. It must shed its old skin to grow. Its purposeful writhing is not sinister but tracks the circuitous and sure path toward healing and fulfillment.

How different are these sensations and perceptions of mine from Call's presumably demented experiences of hearing voices? Do you assume I'm also demented because I inherited the genes for it? I assure you—and I believe any clinical test would confirm it—that I know the difference between imagination and reality. I'm not hallucinating.

Are we to dismiss the information Call received from the voices because, at those times, he supposedly couldn't distinguish fact from fiction? He accurately predicted my mother's suicide. He seemed to know when members of the family were ill or in distress. Even when he'd been written off as a missing person, he returned to our house on Chanticleer numerous times. Yes, Dad assumed Call came back because he needed money. But did Call also sense it was time to check up on us? After he came back from his long disappearance, Call seemed exquisitely sensitive not only to my problems and moods but also to my daughters' life challenges.

Wisdom may be no less valuable because it comes from someone who is in an altered state. I don't have to look beyond my childhood Sunday-school lessons to find examples. Moses got instructions from a burning bush. Saul's life was changed when a brilliant light shone down on him on the road to Damascus. The entire Book of Revelation seems to be an extended and highly complex hallucination visited on the prophet John when he nearly froze and starved to death in a dark and dank mountain cave as sea storms raged all around him on the Greek island of Patmos.

Now, some of the faithful apparently believe that the "age of miracles" is over. They contend that God doesn't speak to people in those ways anymore.

I find that impossible to believe.

There are miracles all around me. Call's visitations to me on the wings of hawks are good examples.

The day after Call passed, I called his friend Stan to discuss funeral arrangements. Stan is a minister, and I wanted him to officiate. As I was speaking on the phone out on our porch, a

Call, thank you for being you. I love you.

hawk alighted in a nearby tree. It started to squawk, which seemed unusual to me. Crows and ravens squawk. Mockingbirds sing. But *hawks?*

The subject of our conversation at the time was what music would be appropriate for the service. Was the hawk teasing us with this raucous attempt at singing?

The bird wouldn't stop. I suggested to Stan a song that I knew was a favorite of Call's. It was one of the selections playing in the earbuds Lauren gave him as he lay dying. It was popular music, not a hymn. Stan, a traditionalist, resisted my suggestion and mentioned a hymn that he thought would be appropriate.

The noise from the hawk grew louder. Lauren, who had been sitting just inside, rushed out and screamed, "Mom! What's going on with that hawk? I could hear it in the breakfast room."

Indeed, the hawk had been carrying on for a good ten minutes—all while I was trying to convince Stan to play Call's favorite music.

Guess who won that argument?

Over time, any sighting of a hawk became significant for me, and I associated them with Call's presence. The most dramatic of these experiences happened the day after Call's funeral.

Jim, Kim, Lauren, and I were all staying at the beach house. I hadn't shared all my insights about animals with them yet. After all, Jim had made that remark about my "dabbling." I knew he wasn't making fun of me. He was amused by—and I think he now admits he was intrigued with—my renewed sense of curiosity.

One thing I had shared with them was my notion about hawks. I had gone so far as to suggest that I felt Call's presence whenever I saw one.

After we'd had our coffee and breakfast, we decided the whole family would take some time to chill out on the beach. As we sat around together beginning to unwind, we noticed hawks circling above us. It was an unusual sighting because we shared it as a family—and because not one of us denied the emotions it brought up. None of us had ever seen that many hawks flying together, circling all at once. We were used to seeing them flying—singly or in pairs—in and out of the marshes. We'd also seen them soaring out over the ocean, where they dive for fish.

On this day, the hawks were flying right above us, and it appeared that they were demonstrating *for* us. The experience was breathtaking. We all agreed that we felt Call's presence with us. I felt strongly that this feeling of reassurance was the message I was hoping and waiting for, and I felt a deep sense of peace.

We got up and took a long walk together, strolling down the beach for a couple of miles. As we walked, we spotted ten hawks overhead, keeping pace with us. The entire time, what touched me most was that all of us were experiencing this extraordinary event, and we all found meaning and joy in it.

Perhaps, I began to think, the hawks represent our angels—or perhaps the deceased members of our family and even our ancestors.

I didn't know for sure—does anyone? The experience was deeply moving for me, for all of us. It's not that we knew everything in our lives would go smoothly or there would be no pain. We were left with a sense of gratitude. We remain grateful that, in ways we don't fully understand, we are guided and protected.

The illness that eventually took Call's life was not schizophrenia but cancer. He was a heavy smoker, and his diet did not exactly consist of health food. His caregivers and I had been worried constantly that Call would injure himself, either deliberately or by accident when he was not in control. It was just ironic that he outlasted all those years of mental torture. He accepted his cancer diagnosis with a calm resolve, and we didn't try heroic measures as his condition worsened. Call even shook the hand of his physician and thanked him for sharing his wisdom!

During Call's final hospitalization, I felt even more helpless than I had when his psych drug treatments had failed. I recorded my fretting in my journal, and I continued to write after he'd breathed his last.

The holiday season of December of 2012 was our first Christmas without Call. It was just a few months after he died. One morning as I sat on our deck in Atlanta, I wrote:

> It's 7:00 a.m., and I'm sitting here watching nature wake up on this foggy day. I wish you a Merry Christmas, Call! As I go to feed the deer, I ask that you give me a sign you are with me today. In years past, one of us would always call the other around 8 a.m. on Christmas morning to chat. There won't be a phone call this morning, so this note will have to be it.
>
> I have been meditating, thinking of you, wishing you would send me a sign, one I can't miss. I believe you hear me. The deer are here. Oh, look, there is a raccoon buried in the leaves over there! I will go get my camera. I want to take its picture. Hah, I am sure you are not surprised by this. Just as I stood getting ready to take the raccoon's picture and it peeked out from between the leaves, a flock of Canada geese flew over me.
>
> Instantly, I knew that was your sign to me! I said, "Thank you!" Thank you for my Christmas gift from you!
>
> Last night I got out the stocking you had last year. I put a note inside it saying, "I love you" along with your wallet. Then I laid the stocking in the lap of one of my Santa dolls. Later, as I was thinking how much you loved Christmas, I thought maybe I will pull out some of the old black-and-white movie footage of Christmases when we were little.

This notion of soul contracts is the spiritual lesson I take from my bonding with Call, along with a way to find some meaning in the intertwined struggles of the Richmonds and the Schapers.

On a practical level, we can think of the soul as an innate moral sense. We somehow know right from wrong—unless the person has an aberration of brain chemistry that alienates him from himself and from all other people. A sociopath does not simply ignore moral judgments. He perceives choices as correct only if they ensure his survival. Like schizophrenia, sociopathy is an altered state. It, too, comes with a gift—albeit chilling—the ability to survive and prevail at any cost.

As a moral compass but also a spiritual one, the soul always knows the way home. It yearns for the source of all life, and this tendency urges us to higher and expanded states of consciousness. We tend toward compassion. The quest for enlightenment uplifts, relaxes, inspires, encourages, and appreciates. Our soul's longings draw us to beauty, which is both ennobling and comforting. We feel contentment when we know that our life choices align with our soul's direction.

For the individual, a soul contract—as Call so capably demonstrated through his love and support of me and my daughters—defines the person's life mission. Herein lies the principle of karma—the soul's debts—and the burning, or fulfillment, of karma as life experiences resolve those debts. But this description of karma is ancient and perhaps too simplistic. It implies that God is an accountant, meticulously recording sins and payments as debits and credits.

A more updated concept of karma is lessons to be learned. Karma is a curriculum for the soul in the school of life experience. The soul yearns to learn.

Moving beyond the mission of the individual, the soul contract also defines relationships and interactions with other souls and the people in which those spirits assume physical form and personalities. Soul contracts are comingled and overlapping. Life paths intersect, cross, and twist around each other—resulting in knotted webs that are seemingly impossible to make straight.

A friend who is a mental-health professional described it to me this way:

> A family is like a mobile that dangles above an infant's crib. Pull one piece down, and the other pieces collide and may

become entangled. The more agitated the disturbance, the messier the tangle. The interconnected and interdependent network of suspended pieces causes all of them to be affected by any stress on one.

As I've said previously, the health crisis of one family member is a problem for the family. It's not just an immediate problem that requires resolution of financial or relationship issues. It's often a problem with the family itself, with its history of dysfunctions and ailments among parents and even ancestors. It is, in the language of the shamans, a *tribal* problem.

In the case of my family, I feel as though I have been at the center of it all. I've been wrapped up in entanglements. I've tried to identify the lessons to be learned. I've ferreted out the truth. I've cast light into the dark places. For some of us, like my parents, those insights came too late. But who am I to judge—as I am still working through this life—whether they succeeded or failed in their life missions and their soul contracts?

I've expressed the thought that evil exists to fuel the engine of creation. The universe must keep evolving. That's a partial answer to one of the deepest philosophical questions. Thinking now of soul contracts, a question just as deep arises: *Do we have free will?*

A person's life story seems to be a series of choices. When my mother was in the throes of her mental illness, did she have a choice about her self-medication? What alternatives did she have in those days? When my father felt closed off from intimacy and affection, surely abusing his daughter couldn't have been his only choice!

What if Call hadn't run away? What choices would have been available to him if he'd stayed at home and slipped more and more into his hallucinations?

What if Jim and I had managed to prevent the abuse Kim experienced? With whatever the forces were that surrounded her and the heritage of her grandmother's and her uncles' mental instability, would she have suffered nervous breakdowns anyway?

It seems to me that I have free will, to some degree. I know I'm going to act as if I do. I made a conscious decision and a concerted effort to help Call. In my heart, I believe I had no choice. That's what I tried to tell my family. But I always thought I had options, and so did they.

I don't know. I don't know. It's another question I may not be able to answer in this life.

The story in this book is derived from the scenes we filmed and assembled in the documentary *A Sister's Call.* By publishing this narrative version, my goal has been to more fully describe my process (there's that word again!). I've told you about our struggles, and I've shared some of the lessons learned.

I write this so that you, too, will consider the possibility that change and growth can begin with a dream. You and your mission become stronger with your intent and your commitment. Your vision unfolds and flowers as you share it with another person who will value, hold, nurture, support, and cherish it with you.

I haven't come to preach, but I'll share a summary of my process of finding meaning in life's difficulties: When faced with a problem, first accept that it exists. Study everything you can about it. The secrets you discover will include all the lies that swarm around the situation, including the legends that support denial. Your family—your tribe—may deny the problem for a while, until it gets worse. Even after they recognize the situation for what it is, they may still deny that the family has a problem—and that the family's problem is rooted not only in the current situation but also in generations of family history.

I've talked about Call's process, which I came to believe is evidence of his soul contract. I found meaning and hope in his persistent effort to keep to his plan, holding to the idea that his life, his soul, had a mission to perform here on Earth.

Wondrous to me was the discovery and appreciation of Call's gifts, which nurture me and my family to this day. It's my fondest hope that our society—our larger tribe—will become more accepting and understanding of the extraordinary talents possessed by people whom we persist in labeling *disabled.*

Acknowledgments

THIS MEMOIR ENCOMPASSES MOST OF MY LIFE STORY, BUT its core narrative is derived from *A Sister's Call,* the documentary I made with Kyle Tekiela about caring for my brother after his long absence. Making that movie was a fourteen-year effort, and I owe a huge debt to Kyle for his patience, persistence, professionalism—and certainly his creativity. And that effort wasn't ours alone. There's an extensive list of credits at the end of the movie, and I thank you all again for your contributions and your support through that involved process.

Even before *A Sister's Call* first screened, I sensed that a big part of the story had not yet been expressed. I wanted to share my intimate thoughts about the experience. That was my motivation for writing this book. I'm grateful to Eda Long, my early editorial collaborator, who helped me get words onto paper. Then, besides adding his insights on my story, coauthor Gerald Everett Jones suggested we use the movie scenario as the spine of the book and supplement it with relevant reflections I'd shared with Eda. Gerald has also been instrumental in shepherding the book project. He helped me set up GreyHawk Media to publish this book, rerelease *A Sister's Call*, and ignite my social media presence at rebecca schaper.com. Amber Konkol has been our able website developer.

Thanks to Gary Palmatier of Ideas to Images for a breathtaking cover and top-tier book design. Robin Quinn of Quinn's Word for Word was our meticulous copyeditor. I'm also indebted to Robin for introducing me to Gerald in her role as an initial book consultant.

Jeff Perlman handled publicity for *A Sister's Call*, and Darlene Chan has taken care of media relations for this book. Thanks to beta readers Cheyenne Cockrell, Thomas Page, Justin Greene, Perry Zimmerman, Sandra Bautista-Lechner (LCSW), William Anthony, and Robin Levey for their reality-checks of the draft manuscript. Memoir coach Roberta Edgar read the beta manuscript and gave us insightful notes.

I want to pour my heart out to the medical professionals who supported Call. These Earth angels include social worker Cathy Gantt, psychiatrist Dr. Sheldon Cohen, and clinical counselor Tracy Newton. I also sought advice from physical therapist Seth Oberst on how he helps clients who have depression and anxiety. As seen in the film, Call's personal friends who welcomed him back with good humor included Rev. Stan Johnson, Rick Farnsworth, and Fletcher Mann Jr.

Wise counselors and advisers informed our book development: soul astrologer Mark Borax; intuitive consultant and spiritual teacher Robert Ohotto; medium, life coach, and clairvoyant Thomas John; NAMI SC board member and transformational life coach Fletcher Mann Jr.; author and holistic health coach Jocelyn Mercado; and Dr. Gregory W. Dalack. I also want to acknowledge my friend Annie Nord for her love and support.

My brother David Richmond has been generous, loving, kind, and indulgent through all of this. Both in the film and on these pages, you will see how forthright he's been in sharing his memories and insights.

For my daughters Kim and Lauren, there are no words. Their heartfelt contribution to this book and to supporting Call over the years is amply demonstrated in their own words, quoted in these pages. And I thank Ryan Owen and Gabe Simpson for being inspiring partners to Kim and Lauren.

To my mother-in-law Marge Schaper, how can I thank you enough for welcoming Call back into our lives? You said from early on it was a "plan from Upstairs." How right you were!

Finally, to my husband Jim, I can never say it enough: You are my rock. You are so supportive, my soundness-of-mind coach whenever I need you. And your words of wisdom help me keep things in perspective.

Rebecca Schaper
Atlanta, Georgia
January 2018

For Further Reading

Mental Illness

Stephen Harrod Buhner, *Plant Intelligence and the Imaginal Realm: Beyond the Doors of Perception into the Dreaming of Earth* (Bear & Company, 2014). A manual for expanding one's consciousness about the natural world, which includes an examination of schizophrenia as paranormal.

Jeffery Eugenides, *The Marriage Plot: A Novel* (Farrar, Straus and Giroux, 2011). A fictional story involving three college seniors at Brown in the early eighties, one of whom has bipolar disorder.

Elyn R. Saks, *The Center Cannot Hold* (Hachette Books, 2007). A memoir about living with paranoid schizophrenia written by an esteemed professor, lawyer, and psychiatrist who is the Orrin B. Evans Professor of Law, Psychology, and Psychiatry and the Behavioral Sciences at the University of Southern California Gould Law School, and who still suffers from episodes.

Tim Salmon, *Schizophrenia—Who Cares?: A Father's Story* (Blackbird Digital Books, 2015). A brutally honest account of the author's struggle through the development of his son's paranoid schizophrenia.

Mark Vonnegut, MD, *The Eden Express* (Praeger, 1975). A memoir of having a nervous breakdown and getting well again by a practicing pediatrician and son of novelist Kurt Vonnegut Jr.

Spirituality and Metaphysics

Mark Borax, *2012: Crossing the Bridge into the Future* (Frog Books, 2008).

———, with co-author **Ellias Lonsdale**, *Cosmic Weather Report* (North Atlantic Books, 2010).

Borax is a psychic and astrologer.

Ram Dass, *Miracle of Love: Stories about Neem Karoli Baba* (Hanuman Foundation, 1995). Philosophical and metaphysical reflections on the life of a guru.

Thomas John, *Never Argue with a Dead Person: True and Unbelievable Stories from the Other Side* (Hampton Roads Publishing, 2015). This psychic's accounts of communication with the spirit world.

Caroline Myss, PhD, *Sacred Contracts: Awakening Your Divine Potential* (Harmony, 2002).

———, *Anatomy of the Spirit: The Seven Stages of Power and Healing* (Harmony, 1996).

———, *The Creation of Health* (Harmony, 1998).

Books on spirituality and healing by this best-selling author, medical intuitive, and mystic.

Robert Ohotto, *Transforming Fate into Destiny: A New Dialogue with Your Soul* (Hay House, 2008). Metaphysical philosophy by an intuitive, teacher, and speaker.

Support Organizations

Canadian Mental Health Association (CMHA)

www.cmha.ca

CMHA influences public policy and health system planning to promote mental health.

Greer Mental Health Center, Greer, SC

scaccess.communityos.org

A division of the Piedmont Center for Mental Health Services (PCMHS), the clinic provides outpatient mental-health assessment, counseling, crisis intervention, psychiatric treatment/therapy, and support services.

Mental Health America (MHA)

www.mentalhealthamerica.net

MHA is the nation's leading community-based nonprofit dedicated to addressing the needs of those living with mental illness and to promoting the overall mental health of all Americans.

National Alliance on Mental Illness (NAMI)

www.nami.org

The largest grassroots mental-health organization in the U.S., dedicated to building better lives for the millions of Americans who face mental illness every day.

New York City Mental Health Film Festival (NYC MHFF)

www.mentalhealthfilmfest.nyc

Established in 2005, MHFF has screened more than 50 films, attracted over 5,000 audience members, and served as a positive voice for people with mental-health concerns.

Other Voices

mchvn.org

Part of the Montgomery County Community for Hearing Voices Network (MCHVN), this organization's mission is to carry a message of recovery, empowerment, hope, and healing to people with mental-health issues.

One Mind Institute

www.onemindinstitute.org

The institute advocates advanced approaches to treating and coping with schizophrenia.

Vinfen

www.vinfen.org

Vinfen provides comprehensive community-based services for adolescents and adults with psychiatric conditions, intellectual and developmental disabilities, brain injuries, and behavioral health challenges.

Discussion Questions

1. Why might it be said that mental health is not just the absence of disease?

2. Why might it limit our understanding to refer to altered states as mental *illness?*

3. What organizations or institutions can have the most transformational impact on promoting mental health?

4. Have you known people who have disabilities whose conditions also gave them special gifts?

5. A basic test of social maladjustment can be whether the person is having thoughts of harming himself or others. Would making the question broader needlessly limit individual freedom?

6. In your own personal beliefs, do you find a difference between religion and spirituality?

7. Many homeless people reportedly say that they would rather be on the street than accept assistance. Why do you think they feel that way?

8. Do the ideas of reincarnation and soul contracts resonate with you?

9. If a person says she's found meaning in life, does it matter whether other people think it's true?

10. Rebecca comments that she believes animals deliver messages to her. Have you ever thought you received information in paranormal ways?

11. Do you experience visions, sensations, intuitions, or perceptions that you can't explain? Do you suspect more people have these experiences, but most aren't able to talk about it?

Watch the Documentary

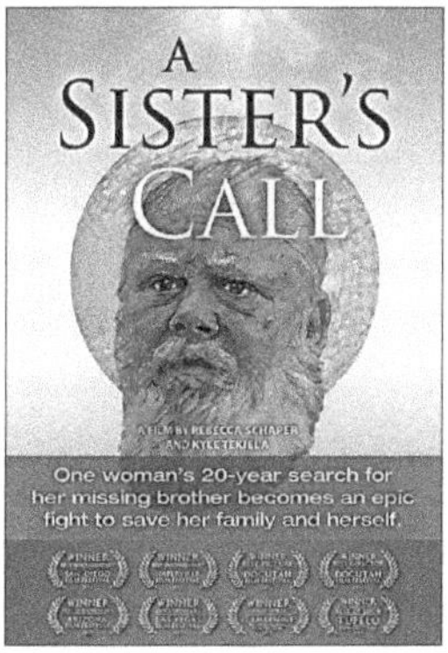

In 1977, Call Richmond went missing. Twenty years later, he showed up on a family member's doorstep suffering from paranoid schizophrenia. Filmed over fourteen years, *A Sister's Call* captures Rebecca Schaper's brave journey of "bringing her brother back." While celebrating his healing, the family is finally forced to reconcile the dark traumas and painful memories of their past.

The award-winning film *A Sister's Call* is available for streaming or download at *www.rebeccaschaper.com.*

Kyle Tekiela (director), Rebecca Schaper (executive producer and co-director)
Produced by Tekiela Creative and GreyHawk Films
in association with Kartemquin Films

A Sister's Call has won many festival awards, including:

Arizona International Film Festival, 2012

- Reel Frontier Special Jury Award, Documentary Filmmaking

DocUtah International Documentary Film Festival, 2012

- Best Documentary
- Best Director

Fort Lauderdale International Film Festival, 2012

- Spirit of the Independent Award, Documentary

San Diego Film Festival, 2012

- Festival Award, Best Documentary

Tupelo Film Festival, 2013

- Festival Prize, Best Feature Documentary
- Ron Tibbett Award, Best of Show

About the Authors

Marion Yarger-Ricketts

Rebecca Schaper is an author, philanthropist, social activist, and filmmaker. (She has such a keen, subjective eye that she calls herself an "intuitive photographer.") With Kyle Tekiela, she co-produced and directed the award-winning documentary *A Sister's Call.* The film chronicles her mission to bring her brother Call Richmond Jr. back from the depths of homelessness and schizophrenia, all while seeking ways to heal herself and her family from the past. Her memoir *The Light in His Soul: Lessons from My Brother's Schizophrenia* recounts the events in the film, supplemented by her intimate personal reflections on recovering from trauma and developing spiritual insight.

Rebecca makes frequent public and media appearances as a spokesperson for mental-health awareness and spiritual development, including presentations to the National Alliance on Mental Illness (NAMI), Vinfen community-based services, the NYC Mental Health Film Festival, Greenville Mental Health Center, the Canadian Mental Health Association, the First Presbyterian Church in Greenville, and the American Psychiatric Association (APA). She is a supporter of NAMI, as well as benefactor of the Great Plains Foundation for African wildlife conservation, a family-assistance program in Kigali, Rwanda, a children's school at the Drepung Gomang Monastery in Bhutan, and the Healing Center in Bali. She is also facilitating the global outreach efforts of the Last Inca Shamans Healing Association of Q'ero Nation in the Cusco region of Peru. She helped sponsor the film *Ram Dass, Going Home* by Derek Peck. She makes her home with her husband Jim in Georgia.

Collaborator and book developer **GERALD EVERETT JONES** is the author of seven novels, including *Bonfire of the Vanderbilts,* and the nonfiction title *How to Lie with Charts.* He is also the host of the *GetPublished!* radio show (www.getpublishedradio.com).